WORKING WITH CHILDREN

WORKING WITH CHILDREN

Assessment, Representation and Intervention

TOM BILLINGTON

SAGE Publications

London • Thousand Oaks • New Delhi

SAGE Publications Ltd
1 Oliver's Yard
55 City Road
London EC1Y 1SP

SAGE Publications Inc.
2455 Teller Road
Thousand Oaks, California 91320

SAGE Publications India Pvt Ltd
B-42, Panchsheel Enclave
Post Box 4109
New Delhi 110 017

British Library Cataloguing in Publication data

A catalogue record for this book is available
from the British Library

ISBN 10 1-4129-0869-8   ISBN 13 978-1-4129-0869-6
ISBN 10 1-4129-0870-1   ISBN 13 978-1-4129-0870-2 (pbk)

Library of Congress Control Number: 2006923438

Typeset by C&M Digitals (P) Ltd., Chennai, India
Printed in Great Britain by the Athenaeum Press, Gateshead
Printed on paper from sustainable resources

CONTENTS

ABOUT THE AUTHOR

Tom Billington is Senior Lecturer in Educational and Child Psychology at the University of Sheffield where he is also Course Director for the research Doctorate in Educational Psychology and a member of the inter-disciplinary Centre for the Study of Childhood and Youth. He continues to practise in child and family care proceedings and is a member of British Psychological Society cross-Divisional working parties in child protection and childhood autism.

ACKNOWLEDGEMENTS

I am indebted to all those who, across the social sciences, have provided inspiration through their work and ideas evolved over decades. I would also thank those with whom I have worked whether in education, health, social sciences or the courts, for their own particular models of dedicated practice. The commitment of colleagues at the University of Sheffield to the principles of social justice has provided an essential collegial foundation, whilst the willingness of our doctoral community to tolerate and engage with difficult ideas never fails to restore and reinvigorate.

My family has once again been sacrificed to such a project – Josie, Matthew, Marianne and Sam – but special thanks are due to Joanne who has worked so hard on the manuscript and who has had to make sense of my often incoherent intentions.

Finally, but certainly not least, this book is dedicated to the lives of those young people, their parents and the professionals upon whom this work relies.

I INTRODUCTION

There are persons who are endeavouring to situate their own lives in preferred stories and to embrace their own knowledge, but who are finding it difficult to do so because of the dominant and disqualifying stories or knowledges that others can have about them and their relationships.

(White, 1989, in Billington, 2002: 38)

As we are urged to contemplate a new era of providing services to children and young people, what are the principles that will underpin new frameworks of professional practice and to what extent will any changes, at root, be either cosmetic or driven by economic considerations?

A particular view has been gaining popularity for over twenty years now that professionals need to find new ways of working together in order to address all the many and various needs of children and young people. The UK government, in particular, has been active in this respect and following its ratification of the *United Nations Convention on the Rights of the Child* (UNICEF, 1989) has produced a vast number of related policy statements, of which the most important in recent years are *Working Together* (DoH, 1998b), *Safeguarding Children* (DoH, 2002) and especially *Every Child Matters* (DfES, 2003) which poses the possibility of change to institutions and professional systems in its calls for workforce reform. Most recent still will be the new *Working Together* document which is currently going to press.

Much of the drive for change has resulted from a steady procession of high-profile child protection cases (Laming, 2003) and clearly any horror we might feel in respect of individual cases and events will not be misplaced. As a result all recent governmental guidance has exhorted professionals to work together across disciplinary and institutional boundaries, primarily to develop professional practices that will prevent the worst kinds of miscommunication and misunderstanding that seem to characterize these individual tragedies. That working together is a *good thing* is a difficult concept to challenge, but developing such working practices on a day-to-day basis is notoriously difficult.

Professionals across different agencies (broadly speaking, Education, Health and Social Services) clearly adopt different practices with different emphases and responsibilities and are answerable to different employer demands. For example, education professionals are being exhorted to enhance the level of basic skills of young people and social workers are similarly exhorted to enhance the levels of protection afforded to vulnerable children. Delinquency and youth offending, however, are sites where the blame invariably falls less problematically upon the young people themselves (see Goldson et al., 2002). The sharing of a common language can be elusive, though as professionals we seem to be expected to achieve a kind of uniformity of approach. While developing a common language might be desirable in many respects, it would be of concern should such a project lead to a stifling of dissent and the discouraging of highly necessary professional debate (see for example Billington and Warner, 2003: 5–6).

Thus this book arises out of both a context and a history in which a government is making plans to change the ways in which professionals meet the needs of children. Many of the issues, however, (or discourses – see Burman and Parker, 1993) transcend national boundaries and globally there has been an ever-increasing scrutiny of young people during the last two hundred years (see for example James et al., 1998; Mayall, 2002). Currently, the focus may be shifting to a major re-evaluation of adult professional practices, systems and agencies, involving all those who work with children across post-industrial societies. To what extent though will any reforms more effectively expose individual children to scrutiny in order to provide better care, or will such benevolence mask the possibility that both government and regulations will be less benevolent? I would suggest that the recent history of professionals working with children reveals two competing and perhaps mutually dependent discourses: firstly, that a young person is in need of adult protection and support and secondly, that a young person is in need of adult instruction, control or even punishment.

A discourse is a set of images, written texts, beliefs, metaphors (and anything else that can be 'read' for meaning) that shape, inform or construct a particular practice or phenomenon.

(Nightingale and Cronby, 1999; 226)

It does not help matters that frequently young people are now spoken of as if they were members of some kind of alien race from whom we have become totally disconnected and at times it seems as though the category of childhood provides the most convenient site for human governance and investigation (Rose, 1985; James et al., 1998). This book is thus born out of current adult anxiety in relation to all our young and seeks firstly to provide a template for containing and processing some of that complexity and secondly, hopes to encourage practitioners to resist analyses which allow an individual young person to be cut free from broader social analyses and understandings. I will argue that current anxieties about our young are in part a smoke-screen for our own adult anxieties – about how we should be in the world, about normality and about our own futures and sense of mortality.

Children and young people as yet possess little political power that is free from adult sanction and they clearly share much in common with all those marginalized groups in society who can be subject to abuses of power (Billington and Pomerantz, 2004). They are subject ultimately to the control of adults and are frequently vulnerable to any adult in their family, school or other government agency who seeks unreasonably to impose their will upon them. Children contribute one of the last discrete categories of population to be formally disenfranchised within western democratic processes.

Unlike other marginalised groups children are often not in a position to enter into dialogue with adults about their community needs and environmental concerns. Despite the current emphasis on involving communities in the regeneration of their own neighbourhoods, young people are still seemingly invisible in decision-making processes. (Matthews, 2003: 264)

As adults it can be reassuring to hold on to or be reminded of ideas of childhood innocence and future potential, not least because we have each known childhood and have thus known something of hope, as well perhaps as that vulnerability to unreasonable adult authority. Currently, however, we seem tantalized by other discourses which demonize young people's resistances and challenges to adult reasoning and demands for good order, for example those manifest in adult anxiety about young people's anti-social behaviour. Many of the causes of adult anxiety in relation to young people's anti-social behaviour are not new, but what is more recent is the systematic targeting of young people as an isolated source of such disorder. Adult coercion or exploitation of people according to their allotted status of 'childhood' has been organized and institutionalized during the last two hundred years, for example in order to control young people's access into the workforce, whether in the nineteenth century factories and mines, or unfortunately in many more recent examples of low-paid, low-status employment. Sometimes institutional responses to young people in the workplace, in families or inside schools have been less than ideal.

Those readers who prefer unproblematic accounts of issues and dilemmas or who want detailed advice about symptoms or disorders are likely to be disappointed here. Similarly, rather than arriving at a simplistic 'how-to' list, my intention will be to tease out exemplars and principles which might be useful across disciplines. The specifics of current practice in different professional domains will not be the focus of this book.

SOCIAL JUSTICE AND THE VOICE OF THE CHILD

A particular response, however, to the potential changes within the children's workforce is sought which will preserve an emancipatory theme in relation to children and young people and will endeavour to remain at the boundaries of social justice. This approach seeks to connect with a longer term historical context for the organized study of children which can be traced back to the origins of the social sciences during the second half of the nineteenth century (Spencer, 1861 [1932]); Galton, 1869, 1883; James, 1890). Indeed historical readings constitute a recurring theme but there are several other themes which are intended to provide a continuity of approach as they become manifest across the various chapters.

One such theme linked to the emancipatory intent is that of the *voice of the child*. Now this concept is a tricky one since it can rather too easily become yet another mantra akin perhaps to *social inclusion* or *working together*, all terms which would clearly in themselves lay claim to being good things. However, sometimes such terms can become opaque to the analysis of complex discourses of meaning and power circulating within them and the manner in which the voice of the child is heard in this book needs some initial clarification.

It would have been possible with this book to have provided an opportunity for various young people to have spoken out proactively. I decided not to do this for several reasons, each of which provides an example of the subtle deployment of (adult) power and authority in the lives of the young. Firstly, the selection of any young person for inclusion here would have remained within my adult gift. Secondly, so too would ultimate editorial control. Thirdly, I might have selected young people whose chosen means of expression would then not have been acceptable for publication and would have required (adult) censorship.

The point here is that at some moment or other I, as an adult professional, would have had the power to take control of the voice of the child. While there are, of course, published examples of young people writing about their own situations, at some point in the process an adult – whether parent, carer, childcare professional, researcher or publisher – plays an influential part in allowing that voice to be heard.

Much autobiographical work is, of course, not only admirable but hugely revealing and informative; vital even, if we are to alter fundamentally the nature of professional-client relationships and for this reason narrative work with young people is encouraged in subsequent chapters. However, notions of *partnerships* can sometimes obscure the crucial issues at stake (of power and control) and not least such approaches can lead us to place the focus once again upon the (individual) young person. It is for a combination of such reasons that I have unashamedly retained control over the voice of any young person who appears (anonymously) within this book. It is an important theoretical point that in making such representations it is the author's voice that is heard and the fragments of the young person that survive do so only with my consent (Derrida, 1975; Lacan, 1977; Genette, 1980; Cooter, 1992; Duden, 1992; also Goodenough et al., 2003).

Clearly, in all societies, adults exercise control of their young and this book does not seek to challenge such authority per se. Rather, what is sought here is to expose those particular ways in which the actions of adults can serve merely to impose a means of control as part of a web of governmentality (Foucault, 1979, in Billington, 2000a; 23) and these ways will either lead to harmful consequences or those which are at best unnecessary.

> Governmentality is the totality of the very particular ways in which the supervision of populations has developed beyond national govern-ments permeating an array of institutions and practices.
>
> *(Billington, 2000a: 23)*

This book, therefore, is about what we do as adult professionals when working with children and examines the principles and ideas which underpin those practices. While the focus is on indi-vidual practices, the institutions and systems provide a context for the emergence of these professional practices and as such both will be considered.

There are various representations of individual children and occasionally their words are cited verbatim. These accounts will be used within a context of adult professional responses inside the childcare system, whether relating to education, health, the law or social services and will lead to opportunities for critical analysis. Such accounts will hopefully serve firstly as exemplars of resis-tance to practices that can be deemed oppressive and secondly will lead to alternative suggestions as to how we can extend democratic potentials.

SOCIAL INTERACTIONIST MODELS OF PROFESSIONAL PRACTICE

That young people and professionals alike operate within social and historical contexts is another major theme running through the book and attempts to isolate either an individual child or adult will hopefully lead to challenge, especially where these would lead inevitably to stigma or blame. An intrinsically *social interactionist* model, broadly conceived, thus underpins these chapters since a failure to locate firmly within this paradigm is doomed to supply an incomplete, isolated and unsatisfying human science.

It is for this reason that another of the major themes which offers continuity of analysis is the nature of the actual communications between adult professionals and the children and young people themselves (Billington, 1995; James et al., 1998; Leach, 2003; Warner, forthcoming). Once again, however, the focus will intentionally fall upon the possibilities for professional work and upon professional accounts as a resistance to the prevailing mode of practice, rather than seek to explore in detail any individualized child psychopathology, for example.

This book deals with issues in ways which are intended to provide trainee professionals from whatever discipline or domain with a healthy criticality which can be deployed in their work and it is for these prospective practitioners that it is primarily intended. In preparing trainee professionals to work with children and young people it is clearly important that new, and indeed already existing, practitioners are encouraged to examine boldly and reflect upon our own practices (Dominelli, 2004; Freiberg et al., 2005; Hoagwood, 2005; Parker, 2005; Goodley and Lawthom, 2006). The potential reorganization of the childcare workforce is an opportunity to consider the fundamentals of what it is exactly that we all do. For example, how do we perform our work? What ideas and theories do we employ? How are ideas upon which we base our advice or interventions constructed? What is the evidence base for our theories or chosen intervention?

Where children and young people are concerned it is especially relevant to consider the ideas we each have about the nature of knowledge, how we think and learn and indeed the nature of human experience itself, for it has been too easy to position a young person only as a potential learner without knowledge and an adult as the *knower* who has moved beyond learning. Scrutiny should also fall not merely just upon the children and young people, but upon ourselves as professionals and upon the bases of our professional practice. In particular, the professional reader is asked to reflect on their own practice by considering throughout the following five question-themes:

- How do we speak of children?
- How do we speak with children?
- How do we write of children?
- How do we listen to children?

And finally

- How do we listen to ourselves (when working with children)?

I would suggest that these questions can form the bases not just for simplistic checklist appraisals of individual professional practice, but also as a means of developing those reflexive and critical faculties which enable us to understand more of what we are doing and to open our eyes to the effects of our actions, for good or ill.

It would be hard to gainsay an argument that children and young people today are more subject to public scrutiny and assessment than ever before: 'Children are arguably more hemmed in by surveillance and social regulation than ever before' (James et al., 1998: 7). Some of this professional assessment activity can lead to immeasurable benefits for individual children; for example, via early health screening and subsequent checks, or else via the effective quagmire of social workers' child protection investigations, or through access to enhanced educational resources in schools. Many of the benefits are real and can indeed represent real social progress. However, there has been a recent explosion in the production of texts written by people who, in the past, have been merely written about by others – the pathologised (see Billington 1996, 2002) – and some of these suggest that there can be strains in the traditional kinds of professional-client relationship (that is, between knower and known).

These five questions I referred to earlier can be applied to all professional assessment work with children and young people for rather than the individual pathology, family presentation or manner of functioning, it is the quality of our professional approach and interactions for which we are responsible. It also involves our own assumptions and beliefs about children which, while apparently secondary, often influence the direction of our work, since they provide the first principles of our professional practice. Clearly we need to be able to challenge, and be challenged, in order to realize in our work with children – our *assessments, representations* and *interventions* – the first principles and values which fuel our investigations and interpretations.

THE BOUNDARIES OF LANGUAGE AND KNOWLEDGE

The notion of 'evidence-based' practice has become a popular catchphrase for justifying professional activity, but any precise definition of this seductive term can be elusive since epistemology is not monolithic. Historically, there are at least two very different traditions of knowledge-making and truth in the social sciences – on the one hand those belonging to a positivist tradition of gathering (invariably numerical) data leading to facts that can be known, and on the other hand those which emphasize the impact of interpretation, process and hypothesis-formation. While the general public often seems to possess considerable scepticism in respect of science and scientists, the academic and research communities maintain their boundaries by according high esteem to positivist research. For example, in the United Kingdom, the National Institution for Clinical Excellence (NICE) suggests a hierarchy of research in which the *systematic review of randomized controlled trials* constitutes the so-called 'gold standard' in terms of research evidence.

> Positivism is the belief that the world as it is given to observation (experimentation, perception etc.) is the way that the world actually is. In particular, the questions that cannot be answered by scientific methods must remain forever unanswered.
>
> *(Nightingale and Cronby, 1999: 227)*

However, whether as teacher, social worker, health professional or psychologist, our professional trades are largely dependent on the exchange of language and there is evidence that communication via language is less than exact (Lacan, 1977). During the twentieth century, an exploration of the nature and function of language has given cause to question the assumptions about the reliability of word meaning and this raises the possibility that professionals working with children may often miss some of the complexity and variability of their own language use and could thus be accused of being non-scientific (see Billington, 2000a: 13).

> word meaning has been lost in the ocean of all other aspects of consciousness, in the same way as phonetic properties detached from meaning have been lost among the other characteristics of vocalization. Contemporary psychology has nothing to say about the specific ideas regarding word meaning. (Vygotsky, 1986: 5)

Another theme running through this book is a concern over issues of power and a belief that too many children suffer disadvantage unnecessarily in our society (Billington, 2003). Much of the clinical data are taken from the author's own practice as a psychologist working in childcare proceedings and prior to that when employed by a local authority as an educational psychologist and also as a specialist in ASDs (autistic spectrum disorders).

The five question-themes posed lead to approaches which rely heavily on the concept of narratives in our work with children and young people. Rather than the individual or their pathology, therefore, the emphasis will be on the way in which young people are represented in professional accounts, the ways in which these accounts are shared with other professionals or the extent to which they are related to the narrative chosen by the young person themselves. Three important critical 'distinctions' will then be made (see p. 158).

Thus the author seeks to build on a tradition of reporting professional case work which owes much in spirit at least to the legacy of such writers as Oliver Sacks (1985, 2004) and R.D. Laing (1960, 1961), or perhaps Donald Winnicott (1971, 1977) or Marion Milner ([1934] 1986). The challenges they made to extant knowledge at the time were important in many respects but were especially important in exposing the chasm between, on the one hand, the scientific knowledge of individual functioning and, on the other hand, the nature of lived experience.

This fracture that can exist between professional knowledge and client experience is a fault-line that will need to be addressed in the construction of new children's services. Time and again in my own professional work it has become apparent the extent to which services and practices have been created and sustained according to professional and governmental demands, rather than by using any sensitive analysis of the effects of our actions upon the individual who is meriting our attention. There will be references to some of this work but once again the reader should not view accounts of individual actions as factual but rather as representations, as they are a means only of bringing critical illumination to the social processes in which all our professional practices are embedded.

Certainly, there has been a 'shift in ideology and practice of the helping professions towards a partnership model which values the clients' perspectives' (Avdi et al., 2000) and recent UK government documents have continued to emphasize this trend (see for example *Every Child Matters*, (DfES, 2003)). The energy for such change was generated initially perhaps by the *United Nations Convention on the Rights of the Child* (UNICEF, 1989). This document is of particular relevance to all young people, especially Article 12 which specifies the right of the child to express an opinion on any matter concerning their welfare and to have that opinion taken seriously.

The demand that democratic principles be extended to all children and young people has continued to grow through research (Barton, 1989; Clough and Barton, 1998; Armstrong, 2003) and in the UK through important legislation (DfES, 2001; DfES/DoH, 2004). There is also a growing belief that knowledge is not confined to professionals but may be possessed by our clients, the *insiders* (Moore, 2000) who could often participate in decision making about their lives.

Whatever the nature of the childcare workforce, in the future professionals will need to be supported in developing practices which can be sufficiently robust to challenge the prevailing consensus in respect of what is known, for without such challenges knowledge itself will die. The new worker, therefore, must become equally competent not only as a practitioner but also as a researcher and critical thinker, capable of intelligently assessing not just clients but of analysing sensitively their own work, the systems in which they operate and not least the principles and foundations of their institutional and organizational contexts.

The material sciences can perhaps more easily distance themselves from political circumstances, but I would suggest that it is vital that the social sciences remain alert to the dangers of overlooking political or economic explanations and replacing them with simplistic biological or psychological accounts. Worryingly, however, while the wider conditions in which a young person's difficulties can be identified, accrue and remain unchanged, it can be difficult for practitioners to connect the individual situation to distinct political alternatives and choices about solutions. Have we been seduced into viewing the divisions within our society as inevitable? I would put forward that a concentration merely on the psychopathologizing of individual young people can permit social inequalities or injustices either to remain invisible or to be viewed as irrelevant.

There will frequently be insufficient space to provide detailed analyses of some of the theoretical issues in the book and on such occasions the reader will thus be provided with suggestions for further reading as a means of achieving an enhanced sense of critical awareness. I would argue that professionals actually rely not just on 'gold standard' research but upon other forms of evidence – such as popular discourses or personal values, for example (Bailey, 2005). The ability to analyse our own theory building, therefore, is an important facet of our work – indeed, it is evidence.

A CHAPTER GUIDE

Working with Children is intended to contribute to the development of professionalisms in which criticality and reflexivity are emphasized in training as a means of developing good practice in accord with sound ethical principles. Not only this, in the future it is suggested that good professional practice will demand that the practitioner is also a researcher and the notion of a 'researcher-practitioner' model for working with children is also recommended. The model of practice implicit within the book, therefore, is of the critical and reflexive practitioner who engages with research issues as a fundamental requirement for evaluating and thus informing their work with children.

Themes operate along a linear axis inside the book and reappear at different times, although each chapter will have its own individual focus. *Thinking about Young People and Childhood*

(Chapter 2) will examine the evolution of our ideas about childhood and will especially consider the ways in which different domains of study and institutional practices simultaneously both prompt and respond to that continuing evolution. The success of a reductionist model of child development will be considered together with those limits which it suggests for the normal and beyond of human functioning and behaviour.

Young People and the Children's Workforce (Chapter 3) will provide alternative accounts to such a reductionist model in which can be located forms of difference, for example, based around discourses of gender, disability, ethnicity, culture or economic disadvantage. The position of children and young people in relation to service policies and practice will be informed by reference to important literature and a template will be provided upon which the activities in children's services will depend.

In *Assessing Children and Young People in Social Contexts* (Chapter 4) it is argued that services often organize themselves around a *within-child* deficit model of practice and alternative arguments are made which emphasize interactionist ways of working with or of assessing children. The notion of assessment as intervention is introduced and the usefulness of the concept of closeness and distance is explored.

Chapter 5 entitled *Representing Children and Young People in Assessments* will contain a further challenge to simplistic models of *ability* or *diagnosis* that currently underpin many accounts of children's difficulties. Professional decision making and representations will be examined once again through reference to the author's own case work and as such the value of a researcher–practitioner model for professional practice becomes apparent.

The case will be further made in *Children Feeling, Thinking and Learning* (Chapter 6) for professional practices which regard as primary a child's well-being as accounted in their emotional life. Contemporary neuropsychological research will be used to challenge simplistic and long-held notions of thinking as an essentially mechanistic form of cognitive processing devoid of emotional investment. As in all other chapters, evidence will be related to case examples from the author's own practice in which a young person's ability to think and learn has been inextricably linked both to their emotional well-being and to their social and environmental circumstances.

Chapter 7 provides a site for consideration of another specific population and will explore issues in relation to *Voices of Children and Young People in Assessment*. Further examples are provided of the richness of young people's accounts and analyses of their own situation. These will be used to expose dilemmas of power, human rights and professional responsibilities.

Working with Autistic Children (Chapter 8) provides an exemplar of the above in relation to a specific psychopathology – autistic spectrum disorders (ASDs). It will be suggested that professionals could use their imaginative and creative faculties in order to more accurately represent the child's human experience as a key to developing more effective and user-friendly services and practitioner responses.

In *Narrative Science* (Chapter 9) the effects upon services and service users of adopting such approaches are highlighted. The theoretical issues which are inherent within the model are utilized in relation to issues of rights, empowerment, child protection and special needs, and once again individual cases are presented. A model for encouraging inclusive practices in accord with the wishes of young people is outlined.

The overall trend in this book is for consideration of the social and historical contexts of professional work in the early chapters and then a gradual move towards discussion and development of practices in which potential oppression for the young person can be minimized. In the final chapter – *Ethics, Commitment and the Limits of Advocacy: Public and private lives* (Chapter 10) – the case will be made for developing practitioner roles which demand critical research and reflexive activities. It is suggested that the practitioner who is required to be an active and reflexive researcher at ease with the principles of critical thinking and evaluation of practice could begin to engage more creatively with children and young people.

OVERALL PRINCIPLES

This book, therefore, is especially intended for that group of people who are about to embark on their careers in any of the children's services (education, health, social), as well as those existing practitioners who are either responsible for continuing professional development within their particular service or are seeking to develop their own practice or indeed research. In particular, I shall attempt to address a specific concern that many current models for thinking about children's own thinking, intelligences and experiences might one day be considered primitive. I am sceptical, therefore, of contemporary professional positions which too easily lay claim, firstly to know and secondly to apportion blame, for a child's deficiency for example.

Our work with children and young people possesses a constant stream of possibilities and dilemmas and this book is intended to help face the challenges with greater confidence and understanding of our own limits within a demanding social world. Here are some of the principles which inform my thinking:

- critical examination of professional practices and relationships is vital;
- power relations exist within our professional practices with children and young people;
- exclusionary processes are embedded within professional practices;
- professional practices can resist exclusion and pathologization;
- pathologies/blame can be mobile, shifting from one individual/ category to another, for example from a child to a teacher, psychologist or social worker;
- individual professional acts occur within collective social practices and thus pose ethical and moral questions at the boundaries of responsibility;
- the minutiae of everyday events can be imbued with many meanings and matters of importance;
- meaning and knowledge are not restricted to the concrete life of words;
- prevailing models of intelligence and ability are unsatisfactory;
- work or meetings between professionals and young people should be viewed primarily as relationships from which the adult cannot absent themselves.

Many of the theoretical principles of this book were explored and delineated in some detail elsewhere (for example Billington, 2000a) and so the reader will often be referred to other sources. In particular, the author is consistent in regarding theory and practice as one, united in the term *discourse* in which the idea and the act are inseparable.

One narrative which has been important in the development of my own understanding of the kind of discourses and dilemmas faced by those of us who work with children and young people is taken from an incident recorded by a teacher many years ago. A girl 'Sue' arrived at a school and for the first six months teachers could barely get her to say a word; she was clearly struggling with her work. One day she entered a teacher's office unexpectedly and stood motionless and could not or would not speak. She was asked whether she had something important on her mind and she nodded. The teacher had the good sense to say to Sue that they would like to telephone the (female) deputy head in order to take further whatever was bothering her. She again nodded her head in acquiescence. The teacher was later to find out that Sue had subsequently agreed to contact with local authority workers (in her case a psychologist and social workers), but the main thrust of this story was that she was never seen in school again. It was said that she had allegedly suffered serious abuse from a close family relative.

Now this was many years ago (pre-Cleveland) and the need for child protection procedures had not been fully realized or certainly not implemented widely in many organizations. Prior to the incident Sue had been thought by teachers perhaps to be just a weak student, her reticence a facet of an overall learning deficiency. In different circumstances an educational psychologist might later have diagnosed her as being an elective mute. Without suggesting that all children with either learning difficulties or elective mutism have been abused, it is clear with hindsight to see that the professional opinion at the time was incomplete and would have been dangerously erroneous. Working with Sue on the basis either of learning difficulties or elective mutism could potentially have been damaging to her.

Thankfully, much of our work with young people is not always so demanding. However, the story of Sue was seminal in my own development, reminding me often of the limits of my own knowledge and the need to appreciate and respond accordingly to the human consequences of the experience of the young person before me because

The art of understanding those aspects of an individual's being which we can observe, as expressive of his [sic] mode of being-in-the-world, requires us to relate his actions to his way of expressing the situation he is in with us. (Laing, 1960: 32)

Whatever position we take in the vast industry of the children's workforce, we cannot so easily be separated from the subjects of our inquiry.

FURTHER READING

Billington, T. (2000) *Separating, Losing and Excluding Children: Narratives of difference*. London: RoutledgeFalmer.

Burman, E. (1994) *Deconstructing Developmental Psychology*. London: Routledge.

James, A., Jenks, C. and Prout, A. (1998) *Theorizing Childhood*. Cambridge: Polity.

Sacks, O. (1985) *The Man Who Mistook His Wife for a Hat*. London: Picador.

Reflexive Activity

Think of a young person with whom you have worked and jot down some persistent recollections and the feelings evoked. Reflect on the reasons for your response at the time and the reasons for your choice of that young person now.

---

2 THINKING ABOUT YOUNG PEOPLE AND CHILDHOOD

'Our science is not knowledge ... it can achieve neither truth nor probability' (Popper 1966: 228). In so far as this conclusion is accepted – and Popper's argument, strictly following as it does the canons of deductive logic, is compelling – scientists are denied the last possibility of claiming their own motives to be purely and simply those of gaining genuine scientific knowledge or truth. (Tolman, 1994: 28)

CREATING DISTANCE

There have often been moments during work with a young person when the organization of a session according to an individualized account of a particular psychopathology ('psychopathology is a term for those practices which ... have flourished in a search for diseases of the mind' (Billington, 2002: 22)) has seemed inadequate, as if something essential or primary has been missed. I have felt that in focusing on the pathology I could miss something of importance occurring in the interactions between myself and the child. Indeed, the interactions between professionals and their clients are now demanding more attention as a location for the investigation of significant social phenomena. Before addressing this directly, however, it is necessary to examine the social and historical circumstances which have encouraged the growth and development of such special kinds of exchanges – which when seen in another way are, of course, nothing other than human relationships.

The professionalized accounts and explanations I have adopted which have framed much traditional thinking in day-to-day practice with young people (for example, relating to problems or *difficulties*), together with the adult decision-making processes thereafter, have often seemed somehow to lack the necessary qualities of sensitivity or depth of analysis (Billington, 2000a). I have thus questioned not just my own judgment but the limitations of the account I have provided in sessions, either with a parent, another professional or with the young person themselves. There has been a lack of creative thinking and the narratives of experience which might identify with more positive human qualities and intelligences could often be ignored in favour of conversations about 'strategies' or 'targets'.

Removed from imaginative potentials and qualities there is a danger that the young person, from the very point of identification as being in need of some kind of special professional attention, can thus become synonymous with their problem or *difficulty*. This can become an unhelpful boundary to professional thinking and intervention, for example seen here in an educational context. 'Whilst the process of looking for within-child factors may be economic in the short term it is also unecomonic in the long term because it leaves the host culture of the school with a diminished set of tools with which to address problems' (Billington and Pomerantz, 2004: 7).

Interventions built on a simple diagnostic model will invariably result in effective treatment within the sphere of medical health, but those professional practices of diagnosis and treatment which promise such precision in respect of physical well-being are not necessarily appropriate in respect of educational, psychological or social issues. However, those undertaking initial training in children's work across the domains can too easily imbibe a diagnostic model which is pervasive and too often organized around the *deficits* of the young people with whom we work (Parker et al., 1995; Billington, 1996; Jenkins, 1998). In practice, the eager adoption of such a deficit/diagnostic model can create a fissure between, on the one hand, the professionalized discourses of a particular psychopathology, whether of a specific emotional, behavioural or learning difficulty for example, and on the other, an understanding of the experience of the individual young person so defined.

In choosing a professionalized account, we can often erect further barriers against the person with whom we are working and perhaps also the felt reality of a situation. There is a distance created between professional and client and the disparity between accounts, for example between those of a parent and their child but also between my own account and those of other professionals, can sometimes be so marked that the differences become irreconcilable and disputes inevitable.

Now the differences in those accounts can sometimes operate to support the respective positions of the various professionals involved, for there are distinct differences in responsibility and focus for example between a medical doctor, a social or health worker, a teacher, an education support worker or a psychologist. How did these differences arise and what can history tell us about the conceptual roots of the various disciplines, which can often become entangled and perhaps provide a source of said miscommunication?

THE NINETEENTH CENTURY – CHILDHOOD IN ITS INFANCY

In contemplating changes to the children's workforce in the twenty-first century, it might be thought irrelevant to reflect upon even a recent history, let alone one which takes us back to the nineteenth century. However, in this chapter circumstances are considered briefly in which those professional domains and the institutions which support them can be seen to have originated in respect of children and young people; in particular, the principles and ideas that underpinned their individual foundation and subsequent expansion. For it is my contention that if substantive reforms to professional practice are to be implemented effectively in the future, we should be able to critique the evolution of ideas about children and young people that have for many decades been informing professional training.

The origins of our current institutions relating to children and young people can be traced back directly to the nineteenth century. Recourse to history shows us that the maelstrom of human invention during that period did not usher in merely an industrial revolution, but also a revolution in how people lived their lives on a daily basis as the very fabric of society and social experience changed for ever. The power of religion to speak authoritatively upon all matters human had been diminishing in previous centuries, but the sheer force of the social revolution in the nineteenth century effected an erosion of that power still further. The new scientific discoveries, new technologies and new social institutions which were being forged in industrialized societies affected the universal experience of what it was to be human (Owen, [1813] 1927; Fromm, [1942] 1984; Hobsbawm, 1962, 1975, 1987; Williams, 1987; Davis, 2002). Interestingly, arguments continue to be made in respect of our own existing social and economic conditions for living (Sennett, 2006).

The quest for knowledge itself became a particular form of industrial activity – as a commodity. The search for new knowledge expanded in accordance with market forces and a whole range of social activities erupted across medicine and the human and social sciences, accorded with the principles of a *division of labour* between the *arts* and *sciences* (the precise moment of schism identified as being 1867; see Williams, 1987). It is at this point that the study of human being became increasingly subject to a positivist enterprise which assumed an authoritative position through its usefulness to government (Rose, 1985).

Prior to such a fracture, questions that occupied fine minds – relating to the nature of human feelings, thinking and being in the world – would not have been corralled so rigidly. Philosophers or writers, for example, could hitherto have been deemed to possess key knowledge about the human condition, in respect of both our inner and external human worlds; concepts which were soon to be articulated in the emerging social sciences.

The drive for more tightly organized modes of inquiry that we now know as *science* became unstoppable, however, and the social sciences eventually were born out of a curious mixture – the adoption of a new approach to knowledge itself and a development of new technologies; as a response to the uncertainties created by the destruction of old communities and new ways of being in the world; and as a reaction to government need to exert control over a new social order (Hobsbawm, 1962, 1975, 1987; Foucault, 1967, 1977, 1979; Williams, 1976, 1987; Rose, 1985, 1989).

The nineteenth century thus became an era in which particular forms of governmental activity were constructed in order to curb some of the worst excesses of the prevailing social conditions through a process of reform. The earliest reforms were in respect of the minimum age at which children could be expected to work (Factory Acts, 1802, 1833). While schooling had long been the privilege of the few, some far-sighted reformers believed that the education of young people could provide an effective buffer of protection against the worst human tragedies (see for example Owen, [1813] 1927).

In the early nineteenth century, however, the education of the masses tended to be regarded still as a rather dangerous experiment and moves to effect this were resisted. Eventually the competing social discourse that *Education is necessary to improve the competitiveness and development of an economy* became overwhelming in its claims to truth and a system of mass education gradually emerged that created a childhood which became a special preserve for discourses of the most fundamental human potentials and even innocence of spirit (Mill, [1859] 1869).

For example, before the emergence of sociology and psychology as domains of knowledge, the boundaries of *childhood* as a discrete population or experience were not so finely articulated (Aries, 1962) and indeed childhood as a concept would seem to be subject to change 'As the dominant social relations of production, family form and the individual's engagement with society have altered so too have the various forms of "childhood" changed' (Goldson et al., 2002: 18).

There were constant demands to address as new, questions which would otherwise possess a timeless and universal quality; for example, in relation to human purpose, potential or mortality. At the very moment when people began to crowd together in urban conurbations, however, there was a paradox in that it was the individual who then became the subject of a particular kind of study.

Biology, medicine and subsequently sociology and psychology gradually codified their institutional activities and became subject to the conditions of the division of labour, that is as separate, discrete domains of knowledge. Education did not offer itself as a new knowledge in quite the same way, but it provided a site for locating key competing ideas about children and young people that have come to underpin social and governmental policy for over a century.

In its wake, legislation and the provision of services led to a more precise and apparently fixed definition of childhood and education came to serve the interests of government, permitting control over access to and removal from the available work-force. Indeed, once the separation of a distinct population – childhood – had been achieved, it became possible to develop and circulate all kinds of supposedly absolute knowledge in relation to young people. While the kinds of knowledge necessary to assist the greater social (economic) good were encouraged, the ways in which the processes operated often overlooked the subtle transmission of social values. *Governmentality* thus went unnoticed.

In particular, psychology became useful to government, not least in its potential to contribute to debates about what might be termed *normal* in human functioning within fast-growing and increasingly diverse, yet globalized, contexts for living. Physical health had become the property of biology, medicine and their associated activities, but there were other threats to the new industrialized conditions (other than public health) which were social and political. Psychology became a vital arm of govern-ment through which could be pin-pointed accurately various forms of deviance – by placing some at or beyond the margins of society. In Europe, the work of Binet and Simon (1905) developed into technologies offering means of patrolling boundaries in the lives of young people (for example, between schools and special schools: see Barton, 1989). The values and beliefs contained within the first psychological tests in the USA had long-lasting effects which expanded globally (Rose, 1989).

SHARPENING THE FOCUS

A dissatisfaction with some of the latter-day social exchanges between professionals and young people within educational set-tings influenced the change in direction of my own career from education to psychology. The idea that I might as a psychologist be able to be more constructive in contributing to the well-being of individual young people, however, was itself challenged by experiences not just in (re-)training but in professional practice. Hard lessons were learned not only in respect of the power of adults but also in the execution of institutional authority that sometimes seemed detrimental to the best interests of young people, whether in educational settings, clinical or therapeutic environments. More difficult still was the possibility of being seduced into professional practices which again invariably seemed constructed in ways which served the needs of adults, rather than addressing boldly the needs of the young person with whom I could be working.

It has seemed that there are certain structures of thought, ideas and underlying principles of practice – *discourses* – which move between situations and contexts and offer conceptual continuity between domains of professional activity. One such discourse which can be seen across different domains of practice is the singular notion of human faculties reduced to – *ability*. That a person's ability, the sum total of their intellectual capacity, can be contained within a simple number has been pervasive across working contexts. There were to be other surprises in store such as the realization that one otherwise respected colleague actually believed not just in such a simplistic view of intelligence, but also in the assumptions and professional judgments that could be made according to racial or gender difference in intellectual performance. It is possible to critique further the ways in which the array of professional practices and services evolved, but it is undeniable that one result of our work with some young people has been to participate in processes which lead to their exclusion from mainstream social life (Billington, 2000a).

The promise of the social sciences in the lives of young people was to identify individuals in supposedly the most scientific and generally economic fashion possible and eventually certain young people began to be categorized according to one prevalent social discourse or another, for example, those with certain prescribed characteristics, psychopathologies, disabilities or difficulties (Foucault, 1977; Rose, 1985; Burman, 1994, 1999; Parker et al., 1995; Billington, 1996; Jenkins, 1998; Bird, 2002).

The scrutiny directed towards children and young people in whatever sphere of their public lives, whether in school or in the community, would seem to have become ever more intense in recent years. While attention in the nineteenth century had first been directed towards the physical well-being of children and young people, during the twentieth century there was a growing tendency to concentrate on the private lives of children, whether located in schools, in their families or in other social contexts (for example, in forms of therapeutic support). This process has gathered momentum and new forms of scrutiny have emerged.

> Once childhood was a feature of parental (or maybe just maternal) discourse, the currency of educators and the sole theoretical property of developmental psychology. Now, with an intensity perhaps unprecedented, childhood has become popularized, politicized, scrutinized and analysed in a series of inter-locking spaces in which the traditional confidence and certainty about childhood and children's social status are being radically undermined. (James et al., 1998: 3)

Psychology has even offered a site of activity which can reveal the *inner* lives of children and young people, providing an invaluable source for competing discourses of mental health and well-being on the one hand and social control on the other (Sinason, 1992; Urwin and Sharland, 1992; Varma, 1992;). Such investigations, however, whether through professional practices or research activities have led not only to a concentration on deviance from the norm – the development of ways in which a young person's difference or *difficulties* can be identified – but have allowed the development also of increasingly sophisticated ways in which the state can intervene and control this young population. At the same time, some unacceptable situations to which young people have been subjected across different environments have gradually been revealed. Individual childcare cases now challenge us with some regularity through shocking but often sensationalized media exposés and at such moments we can be invited to identify with any innocent child victim.

Frequently media coverage encourages us to blame those professionals who were unable sufficiently to protect such a child. On the other hand we are now sometimes compelled to consider the child as perpetrator and such cases in particular cause great confusion, as we grapple with ideas about *good* and *bad* in children which are immensely difficult to reconcile in simplistic models of human functioning. Certainly, the evidence of accounts provided by child professionals suggests that we are pushed to the limits of our competence in cases where we are left to explain what we secretly fear might be lurking within us all – *the beast within*. In the UK, the case of James Bulger perhaps imprinted itself most strongly into the public consciousness in this respect.

Indeed a series of tragic cases in the UK over decades has shaken the public's confidence in our childcare agencies. Orkney and Cleveland, for example, are place names which have become synonymous with the perceived failure of social care systems. Perhaps the final straw for the British government was the recent case of Victoria Climbie, in which blame could no longer be contained within the alleged individual incompetences but spilled over into criticisms of the institutions and systems which had for decades served the needs of government (Laming, 2003).

Divisions between services had hitherto seemed to be effective in allowing government to have at its disposal a range of resources, sufficiently flexible to be deployed differentially according to specific circumstances. For example, while in the nineteenth century restrictions on children's employment status could be imposed according to economic laws, education emerged subsequently as an indispensable site for control which was beneficial both economically and socially in its effects.

To many of us, education has been a way out of economic deprivation or a chance to discover opportunities, while for others it has become a site in which restrictions could seem to be placed on individual potentials. It was not long before the nature of educational provision had to be formalized if the system was truly to manage vast numbers of children, although the possession of economic wealth continued to allow access to a different and privileged route through education. However, it was the new technologies of *rank, category* and *measurement* (Foucault, 1977; Billington, 2000a) which allowed restrictions to be placed on (invariably) economically less-fortunate populations, whilst allowing exemptions from a *norm*-based basic skills curriculum for those who were able to pay for these. Little seems to have changed in this respect.

THE CHILD AND THE PARENT

Other historical events had a significant impact in adjusting the position of children and families in society at large. For example, the two World Wars in the twentieth century ushered in further social change and a demand for flexible responses, both social and economic. As stated by Dowling and Barnes 'We all need to be aware that images of "motherhood" are in constant social negotiation and reconstruction through the images created by government policy-making and the kind of debates this generates, as well as by journalism, the media and by mothers themselves' (2000: 18).

Much of the rationale for changes in social policy during the twentieth century in Great Britain was provided by the social sciences. Prior to the Second World War, for example, women's employment possibilities were largely restricted to poorly-paid work and the prevalent discourses supported a very particular kind of family unit – father as provider, mother as carer plus dependent children (Riley, 1983). During the Second World War itself, however, women were needed to work in the factories. At the end of the war they were excluded again in order to make employment space for returning men. Was it coincidence that at this very point in history the mother-child bond then became a principal focus for research and professional activity in the social sciences? Certainly attachment theory (Bowlby, 1969, 1994) was an extension to knowledge which was at the least a convenient means of upholding government social policy, as women were exhorted to leave the factories and return to being housewives and mothers. Once safely back in their homes, women were often subject to scrutiny and assessment in respect of their ability to care for their children.

While it is certainly not my intention here to challenge the primary principle of the need to protect children, the process in practice can throw up some anomalies. For example, frequently I am asked in the course of daily practice in childcare proceedings to assess the nature of parents' commitment to their children and the nature of those family relationships. The skill and intensity of parental engagement with children are observed at family contacts and I am often left to compare and reflect upon my own family situation. In one case, a single mother whose four older children had been taken into care was allowed a trial rehabilitation with two of them (Paul and Sammy). When she subsequently wanted to put the older of the two returned children into a holiday play scheme, she was criticized as if this were somehow evidence of a lack of commitment on her part and as such an argument was deployed to suggest a failure in rehabilitation.

In my own situation, however, both I and my partner have essentially rewarding employment and regularly place our children into such schemes with impunity. Indeed our own children can spend many days outside our orbit, for example in (an excellent) nursery and engaged in a variety of other activities. Economic and educational status, therefore, can seem to provide a defence against the kinds of arguments sometimes deployed in case work to denigrate a mother who is not in possession of such material resources. The effects of economic, educational and social capital in underpinning the values and practices of services thus cannot be overlooked (Bourdieu, 1990).

While sociology continues to provide a site for investigating such social phenomena with some success and insight, psychology has effectively allied itself to another kind of authoritative knowledge-making by an increasing recourse to quantitative methods based on a positivist tradition of research and practice. Through measurement, initially of intelligence for example, a whole range of categories and psychopathologies have been sustained and these have been framed in legislation, while at the same time permitting the development of further refinements and representations against which any individual could be located: 'Psychology, unlike sociology, never made the mistake of questioning its own status as a science and, in the guise of developmental psychology, firmly colonized childhood in a pact with medicine, education and government agencies' (James et al., 1998: 17).

LOCATING INTERVENTIONS

Health has provided one site in which issues could be located, defined and addressed and clearly physical well-being and specific medical conditions (for example epilepsy) have warranted very particular responses. Some categories have proved to be less durable, however, sometimes on account of social change and sometimes due to improvements in social conditions. For example, it is rare for any young person now to be diagnosed as *delicate* which had once been a defined condition under legislation.

Physical disabilities in particular have provided a convenient site for locating child *deficits* and whether these lie within hearing, vision or other kinds of physical manifestation, children have been subject to medical assessment and intervention which have often in the process transformed their young lives to positive effect. However, in recent years despite the very efficacy of some of those treatments some people who have been subject to such intervention have begun to articulate a number of concerns, mainly relating to the ways in which long-established professional practices could now be seen to have infringed upon their individual and democratic freedoms (see Chapter 8).

In receipt of such services people had not only accessed positive medical treatment but had also been part of a process which had somehow encouraged the development of discourses associated with deficit. It has become apparent that in the act of intervention the boundaries of normality can be reconsidered and reconstructed and such processes of identification and diagnosis continue, creating new categories as never before. For example, pathological avoidance *disorder* and attention deficit/hyperactivity *disorder* are relatively new conditions, while ever more sophisticated refinements are made to existing categories for example in relation to more precise definitions between degrees or kinds of autistic spectrum *disorders*.

At one level this could be regarded as scientific progress. However, while normality would seem somehow to be linked by alchemy to a standard distribution curve, statistical evidence is beginning to amass which would suggest that, taken together, over half the child population might now be expected to experience a pathology at one time or another before they leave school. These include conditions such as ASD, ADHD, behavioural, emotional or learning difficulties and more besides. Indeed, it might almost be thought *de rigeur* to have a psychopathology: 'Lifetime prevalence of disorders during childhood and adolescence has been estimated by Reinherz et al. (1993) ... Overall, 49% met criteria for at least one disorder during this period' (Roth and Fonagy, 1996: 264).

More generally, the assessment of children and young people would now appear to be reaching epidemic proportions as every aspect of life from birth onwards, and in some cases almost from conception, can be subject to a scrutiny which could be described less positively as surveillance.

New technologies of measurement have been devised and applied not just in relation to medical matters, but in virtually all those other matters relating to education and social care. Paediatricians, health visitors, nursery staff, teachers, social workers, physiotherapists, occupational therapists, speech and language therapists and psychologists both clinical and educational are just some of those who might have cause to intervene in the life of a young person. While there is no massive or compelling evidence to suggest that the vast bulk of this activity is not beneficial to young people, it behoves professionals to consider the new *insider* accounts written by those who have been in receipt of such services. Such accounts reveal the boundaries of normality as the extent and scope of difference become couched in more negative terms – as deviance. As such we live and work now according to an industrialization of difference which at times can lead not only to effective support or treatment, but also to the inculcation or transmission of social *stigma*.

It has become increasingly apparent, however, not only that professional representations can be incomplete, but in some cases have been misleading in their adherence to an array of solely negative discourses (see Chapter 8). At such points doubts must then resurface about the neutrality of professional practices (Young, 1989).

CARE AND REGULATION

To what extent will the organizational premises of a new *children's workforce* allow or even encourage resistance to a deficit model, as well as challenges to the imposition of social stigma which so often presents itself as permanent, both educationally and socially? Such services might, of course, lead to an homogeneity of professional response, the value of which is as yet unproven hypothesis. Certainly the stifling of dissent could be dangerous.

In *Children at the Margins* (Billington and Pomerantz, 2004) I represented Callum, a boy who had become subject to the scrutiny of childcare and educational assessment procedures. In his case, I suggested that while those assessment procedures could well have served to compound his social isolation and render him further vulnerable to the imposition of social stigma, it had been the commitment of a personal support worker who had toiled ceaselessly and with great skill to provide exactly the kind of response necessary in order that social exclusion and stigma could be challenged and resisted. While historical and social analyses are intrinsic to an understanding of contemporary professional practices with young people, Callum's example showed that as individuals our responses are not pre-determined and we are, therefore, not impotent. However, if we truly seek real change on a broader scale we will need to reconsider some of the underlying principles of our current institutions and practices. In particular, we will need to find different ways of representing young people, as currently

> In our collective work we can become overly familiar with the negative processes associated with voices which are not sought out, heard and comprehended. (Billington and Pomerantz, 2004: 7)

More than this, however, we need to devise an alternative language which is based not on deficits but on assets because

> pathology uses a language that constitutes deficit. This deficit language is one of 'less than', disability, incapacity, inadequacy, and incompetence, it is a labelling of damaged goods. It renders its subjects as passive and mitigates against their taking action in their lives against a problem that is put down to physiology. (Smith and Nylund, 1997: 290)

Is it possible to devise services which provide genuine help and assistance to young people without incurring punitive consequences, either material or psychological? Is it possible to help a young person or perhaps allocate a category without simultaneously implanting a stigma?

FURTHER READING

Foucault, M. (1977) *Discipline and Punish: The birth of the prison*. London: Allen Lane.

Hobsbawm, E. J. (1962) *The Age of Revolution 1789–1848*. London: Sphere.

Hobsbawm, E. J. (1975) *The Age of Capital 1848–1875*. London: Abacus.

Hobsbawm, E. J. (1987) *The Age of Empire 1875–1914*. London: Abacus.

Rose, N. (1989) *Governing the Soul: The shaping of the private self*. London: Routledge.

Williams, R. (1987) *Culture and Society*. London: Fontana.

Reflexive Activity

Imagine a time from your own childhood when you were able freely to exist outside the orbit of adult authority. What were the social and environmental contexts of the situation? Would such contexts be possible now? If not, what do you consider might be the implications for children today?

3 YOUNG PEOPLE AND THE CHILDREN'S WORKFORCE

The differences of degree within his [sic] own species are of little significance compared with the possibilities of self-knowledge which would be occasioned by an encounter with a creature of similar structure but different origin. (Jung, 1957: 32)

LESLEY

'Lesley' was referred to me many years ago by her headteacher when I was working as a local authority educational psychologist. She had only recently entered the school and indeed the family had moved together from another area many miles away – Lesley, her siblings and her mother. She was in her reception year but was considered to have both learning and behaviour difficulties and the Special Needs Co-ordinator in the school (SENCO) wondered whether she might have ADHD. Lesley's mother (Mrs L) also suggested that her daughter's problems would not have been helped by a recent marital break-up. This was not an unusual case for this particular school save that the children referred were generally boys.

During my work with Lesley it was easy to see why experienced staff had arrived at their own particular conclusions and ways of representing her. I should make the point here that *representation* is a term which I find preferable on a number of counts. Firstly, in this case *representations* more accurately reflects the situation in which, unlike diagnosing a simple physical condition such as measles, there could be different ways of describing Lesley and her *difficulties*. Secondly, avoiding a conclusive diagnostic category would allow that, quite apart from the number of possible alternatives, the eponymous difficulties could perhaps more accurately be regarded as applying to the experiences of those members of staff who were dealing with her. Thirdly, it seemed to me that I could have chosen to deploy other descriptions of Lesley, for example as 'vulnerable' or 'distressed'.

'Vulnerable' is now a much-used term which has become less than precise in its meanings. In Lesley's case, I used it to indicate that she seemed to possess a quality or manner which I interpreted as evidence that she had been through some kind of distressing experience. Was this mere *projection* on my part or was there substance to a hypothesis that it was this experience which underpinned all Lesley's other difficulties? At the very least the term 'vulnerable' could be employed in discussions with staff, to begin with to put some distance between Lesley and those difficulties and thereafter to elicit some sympathy from those working with her – as opposed to condemnation.

> **Projection**
>
> 'operation whereby qualities, feelings, wishes or even "objects", which the subject refuses to recognize or rejects in himself [sic], are expelled from the self and located in another person or thing'.
>
> *(Laplanche and Pontalis, 1988: 349)*

So what was the nature of the evidence? I asked to see Lesley's mother again and began to discuss my ideas. Mrs L seemed articulate and caring and it was not long before she was describing not so much a marital breakdown, but a desperate overnight flight from a hellish existence in which she had suffered years of violent attacks by the father of her children. Following a previous attempt to escape she alleged that this man had subsequently tracked her down and now she was trying to start her life yet again.

Aha – I was right. And how gratifying to find evidence which supports one's own chosen hypothesis. However, more importantly, for Lesley those years of seeing her mother assaulted and in total disarray, both physical and emotional, had not only had profound affects on her own well-being, but had made it virtually impossible for her to think of schooling as important. She simply had more pressing matters to contend with. Had Lesley memories which she was struggling to suppress? Could she have thought her mother might die during the assaults? Or was she even contemplating her own mortality? More than one five-year-old child has voiced such profound thoughts during work together (see Chapter 9).

The (quantitative) evidence that witnessing violence between loved ones can have a profound impact upon the whole of a child's sense of well-being (educational, emotional, psychological, social) is only recently being compiled and amassed (Alexander et al., 2005). In preparing for this book, however, I had cause to review 100 assessments of young people which I had recently conducted under Children Act legislation (private and public law). I discovered to my surprise that in no fewer than 90 per cent of these cases there were reports (usually confirmed by the young people themselves) that there had been physical violence between their parents (almost without exception male violence upon a female partner). I am now shocked not just at the discovery but at my own surprise at not having previously realized the extent of the evidence. Without any control group there is simply no way of estimating whether this would generalize to all children, either those who are involved in such proceedings or those who are not.

Resistance to social exclusion has often been a paramount objective in my work although not exclusively so, and as was often the case I suspected that Lesley's referral from school had been received as a prelude to conferment of the Last Rites – or rather, before she was to end this phase of her school life and be moved on to another place. Such referrals often caused me to ponder whether my involvement held any great hope of retrieving a situation. Indeed, intervention often seemed to be used as justification for the removal of a child; via a set of coherent arguments of course, since it supported a view that school could no longer be expected to cope with a young person. In this case Lesley, since she needed specialist support and help.

She did need help, but I did not see a behavioural difficulty I saw distress. There seemed to be no evidence, however, to suggest that any pain would be alleviated more effectively by moving her again to yet another alien environment; this time separated from her siblings, outside of the local community and even further away from her mother. Any category at such moments (in this case 'behavioural difficulties') can present as a euphemism; designed to massage professional anxieties and responsibilities, not only as a means of defence against the perceived pain of the young person, for example, but also as a guard against the feelings provoked by self-knowing participation in an act of social exclusion. The evidence that children necessarily do better elsewhere is not to be found.

I chose to employ an alternative discourse with staff at the school – of Lesley as a vulnerable girl, a victim. While this too can be problematic, in discussions with the headteacher I created representations which could be described as less scientific perhaps but more humane, for I chose to represent Lesley not through using discourses of learning or behaviour difficulties or of ADHD, but through narratives of human experience. I then deliberately chose to expose members of school staff to some essence of the frightening feelings with which Lesley would be coping as a result of her experiences, in order that any decision to expel her would not leave them immune to the emotional consequences. This seemed a brutal tactic.

A period of resistance then began where I provided members of staff with as much support as was within my gift in order that they could attempt to hold on to Lesley before rejecting her too hastily. Clearly, on a day-to-day level it was the school teachers who would be suffering the consequences of the intervention; they would be sharing with Lesley, at secondhand, some of the consequences of those early family circumstances which I had by now deemed so distressing to her. After a few weeks, the situation as described to me thankfully began to ease and eventually work took me elsewhere. The teachers had proved able to offer Lesley *good-enough* relationships which contained her emotional disarray (Winnicott, 1971; Bion, 1970).

Should the reader now detect simple self-satisfaction then I have failed to contextualize the situation successfully since my own position was privileged, surrounded as it was by a number of structures and defences which allowed me to keep at bay a too uncomfortable reality. Teachers, in contrast, have to endure the distress of such children for long periods each day.

Three years later (covering a different referral zone) I received a request from another school which took me by surprise – it was Lesley again. She had evidently been excluded eventually from her previous school and along the way had acquired that diagnosis of ADHD (Attention Deficit Hyperactivity Disorder) and was now taking medication. Adult resources had gradually been worn down and presumably in the eyes of staff such a diagnosis would not only relieve them of some responsibility, but would perhaps provide a helpful explanation to Lesley and her family in which it would be the medical condition that was deviant – not her.

This separation however between a child and their pathology is double-edged. While such a diagnosis would indeed allow the participants some space, it would also in the process leave the child subject to (potentially adverse) professional opinion and decision making. Clearly, access to medication could be seen by some as a valid course of action and while I would disagree with this in many cases, which of us has not sought to defend ourselves against a human tragedy (Sinason, 1992)?

It is likely that many of us would have chosen to represent Lesley's *difference* in ways according to our particular professional training and experience, whether this be in education, health, the law or social services. What lies behind the differences in professional accounts and at what points do we either converge or diverge? In order to illuminate this I shall again refer to a contemporary history of human difference.

STIGMA

During the last one hundred years increasingly various professions have undertaken to provide the means for patrolling the boundaries of what is normal in childhood. While teachers were the first professionals to assume this role during the nineteenth century, psychologists in particular began to provide an empirically-based scientific approach in which the child was positioned as 'an object in nature' (Warner, 1897). Sometimes, however, rather than science it was technology which provided the focus for professional activities. Indeed, the implications of such an argument support a critical observation that it is technology and not science that has permitted a social quest for the *normal,* in order that stigmatized differences in the form of anonymised populations or categories can be controlled, regulated and made subject to economic and political controls. Such arguments can be difficult for professionals to accept since we are better trained to look elsewhere when constructing our work practices.

> Developmental psychology has structured the standards and even the forms of modern state intervention that accompany welfare policies or protection and care. Acknowledging these issues means going beyond the representation of developmental psychological research as scientific and benign in its effects. (Burman, 1994: 2)

It has also been argued that

> the idea of developmental psychology has had a greater influence on the way adults think about children than any specific findings of developmental psychologists. (Matthews, 1984: 31–2)

While the processes in which such populations and categories are organized can lead to positive outcomes, I would also suggest that they can possess consequences which are far from benign as within the professionalized practices of social regulation can be found the stigmatizing discourses of social disease. In particular, the allocation of an individualized psychopathology to a child, whilst sometimes effective in accessing important resources, can nevertheless permit the location of a stigma which can have lasting social and economic consequences for the recipient (for example living with professional attributions following diagnosis).

These are not new arguments. While services for children and young people have often been created with the best of all possible human intentions, they have simultaneously sometimes concealed mechanisms by which the stigma of social disease can be transmitted across situations. The history of special educational needs has provided one such convenient site. If we are not careful, therefore, children's services can thus possess a congenital defect consisting of the maintenance and indeed propagation of social stigma – social disease.

CONFINEMENT

Whilst the practice of confining diseased populations has a long history (see for example Foucault, 1967; Rose, 1985), during the eighteenth and nineteenth century colonies of the physically diseased were gradually supplemented by new colonies for the socially diseased. The technologies of confinement which were trialled in the new prisons and hospitals were further extended in order that other identified populations such as poor people, for example, could be confined in the new workhouses of the nineteenth century.

During the seventeenth and eighteenth centuries, large populations began to be identified as 'abnormal' – the physically sick, the unemployed, the criminal and the insane. During the nineteenth century these processes were extended to the lives of children through, for example, legislation in child employment and education. Furthermore, some of those institutional practices which had been developed in the prisons, hospitals, asylums and workhouses came to be adopted by professionals in the new schools which were springing up to accommodate the large numbers of children (for example, lining up before class, classification according to ability, subjection to authority). Indeed schools often seemed organized not necessarily to facilitate learning and creativity, but to facilitate orderly regulation and production – much the same as the character of the nineteenth-century factory.

Foucauldian accounts of history can make uncomfortable or irritating reading for committed practitioners. We will have chosen our professions no doubt for the best of motives, perhaps for example through a willingness to help those less fortunate in life than ourselves, by genuine human kindness or else a generosity of spirit. To Foucault, however, these are the human resistances which are made available within contemporary social power relations, opportunities which will continue to present themselves.

Training for professionals who work with children, whilst acknowledging the liberal discourses of help and care (or resistances), can obscure to its novitiates their performance of regulatory practices, for how else could the processes of social exclusion and confinement continue to operate and expand so effectively? In order to fulfill our disciplinary duties, however, it is expected that as well as providing genuine help and support we might also need to achieve the following outcomes: we must

- access the failure by some children to achieve those particular behaviours which are deemed desirable within the social order;

- represent those failures as individual;
- allow the economic circumstances, which make possible or likely that failure, to remain hidden and unchanged.

TECHNOLOGIES

Our lives, increasingly, are directly affected by activities that are generated under the banner of 'science' and which are applied through various technologies. For many of us in Western countries, these technologies continue to enhance our physical well being; for example, through changes in medical treatment. I suggest here, however, that history can help us to hold on to the understanding that there are aspects of human nature with which science is less certain; for example, regarding qualitative aspects of human nature – human sentiments such as generosity, compassion or feelings. (Billington, 2000a: 60)

In psychology technological concepts have largely been dependent upon the development of statistical models and the normal distribution curve has provided opportunities not just to assist with the segregation of children, but also a means of hiding their individual identities: 'The capacity of any individual could be established in terms of their location along that curve; the intellect reduced to order ... Binet transformed it from a technique for diagnosing the pathological into a device for creating a hierarchy of the normal' (Rose, 1989: 138–9).

Foucault identified three technological concepts that have been embraced in order to facilitate not necessarily the learning but rather the regulation of children. These key regulatory concepts developed in order to regulate children in the most efficient and effective manner are *rank, measurement* and *category.*

In the eighteenth century, *rank* begins to define the great form of individuals in the educational order: rows or ranks of pupils in the class, corridors, courtyards; rank attributed to each pupil at the end of each task and each examination; the rank obtains from week to week, month to month, year to year; an alignment of age groups, one after another; a succession of subjects taught and questions treated, according to an order of increasing difficulty. (Foucault, 1977: 146–7, original emphasis)

Foucault allows us to see that whilst 'rank' acted as a fundamental means of organizing children's lives, so completely has it become immersed within our culture and so effectively have we been trained in its application that today we have to strive to question either its validity or relevance as a concept or even recognize its presence, for example within educational settings. An historical account, however, can help us to conceive of a time when the institutionalization of rank would not have affected the lives of children in the same way, thus allowing us to reflect upon our contemporary professional practices and what we might seek to change.

The importance here of articulating the origins of such a simple principle is that the use of rank has become one of the building blocks upon which the whole system of child assessment continues to be built. Education as well as the additional project of developmental and child psychology have been built upon an implicit tendency to rank children in order. New technologies continue to be generated which can *rank* children with greater sophistication according to their *abilities* or intelligences, whether educational, cognitive, behavioural and, more recently, even emotional (Gardner, 1983; Goleman, 1995).

A Foucauldian reading, however, can allow us to see that whilst such practices claim an a priori knowledge regarding individual children, they are but transient social activities belonging to a particular historical and cultural context. In any case, it could be argued that the 'classificatory coherence and consistency are in the eye of the beholder' (Jenkins, 1998: 223). While such analyses should allow professionals to assume a caution about our activities, which is in keeping with the principles of the scientific method, the application and receipt of any diagnosis will intercede in the lived reality of the participants and as such cannot be dismissed as mere relativism.

In order to rank children, however, we need first to *measure* them in some way and in western social science this has been achieved by stat(e)istics (the *science of state*; Rose, 1989). The measurement of children – their learning or behaviour – is a core activity for many of us who work with children which helps us to restrict the government complexity, for it is through measurement that children's lives can be reduced to the smallest number of characteristics in the shortest time available. Indeed, this measurement can operate in ways which will deny the individual any identity whatsoever.

TESTING CHILDREN

The industry which supports the testing of children is massive, as can be seen in publisher catalogues. The 11-plus, School Certificate, GCEs, CSEs, A levels and then GCSEs have all sought to control the flow of children as they move between one sector of education and another. More recently Standard Attainment Tests (SATs) have been adopted across the age-range and increasingly the age at which children's performance can be measured is being lowered by whatever means, for example the use of pre-school check lists has become widespread.

The psychometric test has long been the main weapon in a psychologist's armoury and its value lies in its seductive promise to reduce any individual to a single figure. Such tests are thus an effective weapon in the battery of assessment techniques which are used to regulate and pathologize children's *learning difficulties* and which can be utilized subsequently to position them against other children according to rank. However, Foucauldian accounts of power relations are complex and these very techniques which are used to regulate children may also contain within them opportunities for resistance.

For example, I have used intelligence tests to convince a court of a young person's mature view as to where they might live, whilst in another forum I have used results from the same tests to highlight the specific nature of a child's reading difficulty, as distinct from other abilities and potentials and not as an indicator of a general intellectual incompetence.

Direct links between the practices generated within services and the differential application of these practices to certain groups of children have long been noted, as well as a lack of professional engagement with the political issues raised:

> Race, sex, disability and sexuality are central to the daily work … These are not in my experience areas of discrimination that are given enough thought or action by psychological services or training courses and are looked upon as issues only dealt with in urban centres. (Jewell, 1991, in Phoenix, 1997)

Measurement and placement in rank order can thus become part of the processes in which a young person's functioning can be categorized not only according to a pathology, but as part of social groupings which are more obviously political. Individual *categories* of children's differences may all be subject to change, however, and previously unknown *difficulties* can emerge.

> Gross categories of (in) competence are not just classificatory categories ... they have been developed as part and parcel of the institutional practices ... bound up in bureaucratic government. (Jenkins, 1998: 224)

As one category is removed from the lists for special attention (for example, *delicate, retarded*) another perhaps unrelated category seems to pop up to fill the space (for example, *hyperactive/autistic*). The social processes through which individual categories of children can be identified and defined, however, are themselves resistant to underlying changes, while emphases in professional practices can shift in a subtle manner according to changing economic demands. These are processes of industrialization of difference through which child assessment practices attempt to step outside history, with the result that manufactured categories organized into various *disabilities* and *difficulties* can suddenly assume the power of timeless, universal, essentialist truths.

PSYCHOPATHOLOGIES AND SOCIAL EXCLUSION

That people have suffered confinement throughout history is not at issue. Unique, however, is the growth during the last three hundred years of a culture in which disciplinary power has been able to infiltrate both body and mind through complex forms of pathology and governmentality. During the last one hundred years, these processes have been extended to children. Too often, science (or rather technology) has provided a safe but unscientific refuge for the emissaries of discipline – 'the minor civil servants of moral orthopaedics ... doctors, chaplains, psychiatrists, psychologists, educationalists' (Foucault, 1977: 10–11).

Analyses here may seem unduly harsh and punitive but are necessary if the regulatory powers we exercize are not to remain unscathed, prior to consideration of those positive and beneficial actions we perform and a retreat to the warmth, security and generous benevolence of our (distanced) professional positions.

Meanwhile, many children are called to account throughout their childhood and for some the wounds may never heal. I would suggest that the totality of the processes which single out individual young people for special attention can bring real benefits – but they can also lead all too easily to stigmatization of their difference and to the following outcomes:

- psychopathologies (or *diagnoses* or so-called *difficulties*) in which stigmatized differences can result in exclusion from existing social relations (for example a child might be required to change schools or home);
- psychopathologies in which stigmatized differences can result in a child being separated from future social possibilities and opportunities (for example a child's future economic and employment chances might be restricted);
- psychopathologies in which stigmatized differences can serve to represent a child as separate from the processes of their social relations (for example it separates the individual child from the environmental circumstances and contexts in which they operate);
- psychopathologies in which stigmatized differences can represent as separate, individual characteristics which cannot possibly exist outside a child's own complex system of unities (for example the allocation of terms such as Asperger's syndrome as a primary means of social identification can separate certain qualities from the other unique aspects of their personality);
- psychopathologies in which stigmatized differences can act to separate a child from their abilities and intelligences (for example by failing to identify possibilities, either inside or outside reductionist definitions, such as *behavioural difficulties* or *autism*).

While it can rightly be argued that children's services are a mark of social progress towards the goal of an enlightened society, we cannot allow ourselves to be oblivious to other factors. On occasions our institutional practices merely act as a means of identifying difference – 'deviance' – in all its forms and thus make it possible to remove from the system those children who are likely to fail according to social norms. The challenge now as ever, therefore, is to create new forms of emancipatory practices which evade such 'man-made' (sic) social failure. In so doing, in order to arrive at more sophisticated thinking in relation to causality, we may need to address the links between ideas of rank, measurement and category ('ability') and a more comprehensive analysis of social disadvantage.

A MATRIX FOR THE TASKS OF CHILDREN'S SERVICES

The systems of social care created over decades are clearly complex and subject to wider social issues. If the children's workforce was just about children it would be relatively easy to establish certain principles – which are indeed the focus of this book. However, there are strong forces at work which provide the foundation, justification and need for particular forms of adult work with children. These forces are related to the economic demands of government and social order. As such, the conditions for a successful economy underpin those services, while at the same time these conditions have to achieve some sort of balance with social and political pressures.

I would argue that all the discourses pertaining to children and young people, the array of practices and professional activities within children services is required to achieve and manage a delicate balance between crucial aspects of social well-being. Principally, child services, care and education are required to be malleable, connecting with and responding to societal meta-processes – social cohesion, social diversity and economic prosperity.

Indeed, education, health and social services are the specific institutional frameworks which are mandated to achieve that balance. Should we merely combine the three institutions into one children's service, we will not necessarily change the need to maintain the social and economic equilibrium. So perhaps what is at stake is whether a single institution might actually achieve its aims more efficiently.

The future of *childhood* and of the professionals who work with young people will not depend merely on the strength of our claims to truth or our ability to orchestrate knowledge. The future will be determined by our ability to assist in that quest for the delicate balance in our society which is to be achieved between issues of social well-being and our political and economic circumstances. This balance is proving, however, to be gossamer-like (or as flexible as it is robust) and future services will depend on our capacity to contribute in a manner which facilitates smooth social functioning according to the following matrix:

Indeed, social inclusion on the grand scale is dependent not on the individual skills of practitioners but on the particular contexts of practice at any time which underpin the emphases between elements of the matrix and thus affect any decision making in the lives of young people.

Clearly, however, no matrix can ever convey the complexity of issues at stake and there are many individual discourses that affect the balance – matters of inequality and social justice such as culture, disability, ethnicity, gender and many more. The web of governmentality is serviced by the agencies of social care and education in young people's lives which in effect allow the latter to act as conduits for the dynamic processes in the matrix above. While it is necessary to understand this *connectivity*, I will now begin to look more specifically at those practices with which most childcare professionals can more easily identify.

FURTHER READING

Billington, T. (1996) 'Pathologizing children: psychology in education and acts of government', in E. Burman, G. Aitken, P. Alldred, R. Allwood, T. Billington, B. Goldberg, A. J. Gordo Lopez, C. Hennan, D. Marks and S. Warner, *Psychology Discourse Practice: Regulation and resistance.* London: Taylor and Francis.

Burman, E. (1994) *Deconstructing Developmental Psychology.* London: Routledge.

Foucault, M. (1967) *Madness and Civilisation.* London: Routledge.

Foucault, M. (1977) *Discipline and Punish: The Birth of the Prison.* London: Allen Lane.

James, A. and James, A. (2004) *Constructing Childhood: Theory, policy and social practice.* Basingstoke: Palgrave MacMillan.

Mayall, B. (2002) *Towards a Sociology for Childhood: Thinking from children's lives*. Buckingham: Open University Press.

Rose, N. (1989) *Governing the Soul: The shaping of the private self*. London: Routledge.

Reflexive Activity

Think of a young person in possession of a particular diagnosis (psychopathology). What was the link between diagnosis and the allocation of services? Could services have been allocated without a diagnosis? What would be the effects of severing this link upon a) professional services and practices b) the young person c) the parents?

4 ASSESSING CHILDREN AND YOUNG PEOPLE IN SOCIAL CONTEXTS

Contemporary research about childhood research with children establishes the limited nature of taking any one approach as the 'truth' about what it is to be a child (Burman, 1994; Mayall, 1996; Hill and Kay, 1997; Alderson, 1995; Woodhead, 1999; James and Prout, 1997) ... Development of appropriate frameworks for research with children may only occur when adequate opportunities are available for adults actively to consult children and pay attention to their experiences and views (Mayall, 1996; Alderson, 1995, 2000; Miller, 2000; Sheir, 2001)'. (Goodenough et al., 2003: 114)

This chapter relies on the premise that humans are social beings and intrinsically so. There can be no situation arising in our lives in which the context for our way of being is other than social. Even when alone or otherwise isolated, we can have no thoughts or feelings which are not in some aspect affected in a primary way by the fact of our human, social being. Certainly, until recently there has been no other possibility that our lives will, from the moment of conception, through gestation, birth and thence to the grave, be lived in a distinctly human environment. Our experience will thus accrue in a fundamental way in relation to other human beings. Now while technological developments suggest that this may not necessarily always continue to be the case, for the time being this book will adopt the stance that the ways in which we negotiate our worlds, through our feelings and thinking, cannot be other than in human, inherently social, contexts.

Since the emergence of the social sciences a distinction between, on the one hand, nature as defined by a biological narrative and on the other hand, our (social) nurture, has provided a site for contests in understanding the human condition and has played a prominent role in determining the foundations of the various approaches, whether in research or in direct professional work with young people. Sociological approaches have tended to concentrate on social groups, while psychological approaches have tended to be drawn to individualized accounts although there are clearly many exceptions to these broad generalizations as well as cross-over points (see for example sociological approaches which can embrace Hollway's (1989) critique of 'rational unitary subjects', or psychological approaches which accept the agency of social groups, such as by gender, sexual orientation or ethnicity).

In work with individual children, it can be easy to lose sight of the broader circumstance of their lives and arrive at analyses which sever the individual from their social and environmental contexts. In the previous case of Lesley, for example, it is likely to have been easier for adults to consider her in terms of psychopathological explanations. To contemplate either her distress or her memories of being the unwitting observer of horrific incidents occurring between her parents, both of whom she might otherwise love and look to for care and protection, would in itself be distressing. The human tragedy seems to lie beyond the limits of professional knowledge and indeed perhaps it should.

However, a lack of acknowledgement of this possibility can (if we are not careful) lead to an under-estimation by professionals across agencies of the experience, quality and impact of children's lived experiences. That children's functioning can be ill-represented by models of developmental psychology is again clear, for example found here in respect of seemingly less harsh circumstances in an educational context:

> It is enough to say here that a girl I was teaching once asked the question "When will I die?" The reader might guess that none of these questions were asked during the literacy hour. (Sedgwick, 1990: 2)

PROFESSIONAL PRACTICE

There have been many examples in my work where the young person has become subject to professionalized discourses which represent their situation as separate from their (human, social) context. While Lesley's diagnosis may have eventually made life more bearable for the adults in her life, there is a growing body of research (for example, Law, 1997; Arora and Mackey, 2004) to suggest that such a diagnosis can have little to offer a young person who chooses to see themselves differently. In his contemporary neuroscientific research, Antonio Damasio suggests the need for caution in too easily arriving at simple conclusions when working with psychopathologies:

> the limits of science: I am sceptical of science's presumption of objectivity and definitiveness. I have a difficult time seeing scientific results, especially as it concerns the mind, does not imply diminished enthusiasm for the attempt to improve provisional appoximations. (Damasio, 1994: xviii)

That a young person might view themselves as being quite distinct from any specific psychopathology (indeed might struggle to recognize themselves as such) can often be overlooked, especially within diagnostic practices even when this distinction can be recognized or accepted. Hollway (1989) suggests by implication that we can fall into a further trap of viewing either the subjects of our enquiry (or indeed) ourselves as 'unitary rational subjects', that is beings whose minds are essentially uni-dimensional in our thinking – logical and consistent – when we know that this is clearly not always the case. We may each, of course, possess various characteristics or attributes, but it can be tempting to assume that these are exclusive and disconnected to other aspects of our functioning, that they are ever-present, immune to change and are the product only of individual capacities or inheritances.

If nothing else, the post-modern frame of mind now demands that we consider the multiple possibilities within ourselves and others. Added to this, one of the difficulties in creating new professional institutions or alliances is that there are well-established but different domains of knowledge. The conclusion here, therefore, is that there can be differences between adult accounts depending on the situation and prioritizations of the individual concerned:

> There is consistent evidence (beginning with Rutter et al., 1970; Shepherd et al., 1971) to show that parents and teachers evaluate the same child differently ... Such poor observed agreement probably reflects three factors (see Kolko & Kazdin, 1993: 1). Children behave very differently in different settings, and some symptoms (e.g. bedwetting, bullying) are only visible in a particular context; 2) the reports of different informants are susceptible to various biases (e.g. parents' reports have shown to be more negative where there is marital stress or

> parental psychopathology; Renouf & Kovacs, 1994); 3) adults are not necessarily
> aware of how … the child is feeling … (Roth and Fonagy, 1996: 272–3)

Many services aimed at young people acknowledge these differ-ences, often dividing their labours between a family and school, care and education (Billington, 2004; Dowling and Osborne, 1985). Such readings, in acknowledging the complexity of young people, their sites of activity and the consequent difficulties of assessing them should not be a problem for professionals, since surely they merely suggest that our practice should be based on a wide range of theoretical resources which can avoid an overly-prescriptive or simplistic analysis.

CONTEXTS

Young people operate in a range of different contexts or 'spaces', for example, which have been usefully articulated as 'the city, the home and the school' (James et al., 1998) and effectively, either urban or rural. Whether the young person understands the collec-tive sense of those spaces in relation to other spaces as we do as adults is not the issue, but rather that there are no other spaces for a young person in which to operate. It is clearly deficient, there-fore, to adopt a starting point in assessment in which we allow that young person's behaviour or functioning to float free from social, environmental, or even historical issues. Our work depends on a range of other factors which one professional or another may or may not have some knowledge of and we should therefore con-sider the totality of experiences in those different spaces, rather than merely focusing on one situation which is perhaps causing a particular professional concern.

For example, if a teacher witnesses either bullying or else autistic behaviours in a pupil, could we assume that the child might always behave in such a manner and across all contexts? How would the answer to such a question affect the professional response? However, if the ways of speaking about a young per-son are repeated often enough, it is likely that a way of profes-sional thinking and talking will begin to emerge in which the young person might ultimately come to be viewed as synony-mous with their behaviour, for example, "(s)he has behavioural difficulties"or "(s)he's autistic."

Where a social worker has been informed that a young person has been using sexualized language or behaviour, this too would be likely to raise different possibilities in respect of cause and circumstance. Once again, even where it proves unnecessary to pursue an intensive investigation, subsequent professional thinking and talking about the young person can be affected by a single phenomenon or incident and this can begin the amassing of 'evidence'. On the other hand, however, for some young people one instance might well be important or significant and it may be, as had been the case with Sue in Chapter 1, that there may have been only one moment for the professional to respond to. Research suggests that there may be many other cases in which sexualized language and behaviour still do not constitute evidence of something more sinister although these are demanding of professional activity. On the other hand, there will be other young people who will exhibit no such 'signs' but yet may be suffering great harm in silence (Department of Health, 1995; BPS, 2004).

The point here is that the issues which must be dealt with by childcare professionals, whether in education, social care or health, are potentially vast and complex. The institutional foundations and practices have largely been based on those principles established within the division of labour and meeting the needs of the market will again impinge upon individual professional decision-making processes. In Lesley's case mentioned previously, for example, the various protagonists – her mother, her teachers and Lesley herself – were not merely dealing with her behaviour, they were operating in a social context in which both the issues and their solution could be defined and controlled by any balance that could be achieved between social diversity, social cohesion and economic prosperity (see p 46).

To what extent was Lesley containable, not just in terms of her behaviour, but in terms of her emotional demands? In other words, could the teachers protect other children, Lesley and indeed themselves? Could the teachers sustain their involvement with her? The levels of emotional investment necessary, together with the imaginative identification with her, would demand much of professionals whose training would not perhaps have prepared them for direct work with such issues, processes or methods. Most importantly, Lesley may not have been contained economically by the school – that is to say, within their available resources whether financial or human?

Assessments of children and young people, however, even when considering the wider possibilities across different spaces or contexts or when eliciting the analyses of professionals in other domains, can invariably focus on a young person in isolation from others. It may be that the families become the targets for investigation, but considerations of the adults involved and especially the institutional contexts within which they operate can be just too difficult or too politically contentious to incorporate any analysis of an individual child. Yet recent inquiries into the operation of our public services would suggest that until we do consider the services we provide for children within those broader contexts, little will be done to advance the needs of our young people (Laming, 2003).

COMMON ASSESSMENT

The Common Assessment Framework (DfES, 2005) is surely helpful in making explicit the full range of a child's needs which should be considered, which are care, education and health. If implemented, the revised framework should go some way both to ensuring that dangerous situations are spotted in some cases, while in others that specific explanations of a child's functioning can be revealed by consideration of the wider context.

However, there are two aspects of the CAF which are more problematic, for there is a danger in the new framework that the opportunities for governmental surveillance will multiply and while this could be a good thing in some respects, for example in order to protect children from harm, history suggests that the consequences of such measures may not always be entirely benign. In some ways therefore the processes of child assessment might, under the guise of protecting children, pose further challenges to the limits of democratic freedoms. At worst the gradual encroachment of institutional practices in the lives of young people might provide a potential means, not only of eroding the boundary of the family, but might reflect broader changes which affect the basis of all our personal relationships.

It is notable in the CAF that while adults fall within the assessment spotlight in the role of parents, there is by comparison scant focus on the qualities of professional actions and responsibilities. While individual professionals can be subject to formal investigatory procedures, for example in relation to ethical practice, there is little consideration of the institutional climate in which these professionals are providing services or any analysis of the nexus between resource availability (financial, professional or human), a child and the individual professional. Seen in light of the Laming report these are significant omissions of analysis, although no doubt the counter argument would be that there are other ways of ensuring the efficacy of services, for example via the government inspectorates, which ultimately should be accountable in democratic processes.

Nevertheless, given that assessment of a child will be conducted at the level of the individual, it is an interesting anomaly that the institutional context and service response are not similarly assessed at that individual level of accountability. This would usually occur only following a serious breach of quality or professional misconduct. Until the quality of professional response becomes part of the individual assessment process, however, difficulties will remain in achieving comprehensive analyses as to whether the systems are operating according to adult need or whether the principle of being child-centred is being achieved as claimed.

The work of professionals is increasingly becoming more subject to scrutiny and there is a range of activities which form part of this process – all kinds of management-directed annual reviews, for example, audits and professional supervision, not to mention an increase in litigation. While investigations in these circumstances are at the level of the individual, in such cases the ways in which the principles and provision of the services impinge on the clients in question rarely form part of the analysis. Such scrutiny, probably quite rightly, is subject to what is ultimately a political process where it is the agencies and government which are held responsible. However, this frequently fails to take account of the effects of such services, delivered or withheld, at the level of the individual child unless special challenges are co-ordinated (for example through complaints, procedures or tribunals).

Assessing the provision and performance of the services available in individual cases would clearly affect the placement of a child within the processes, for they would no longer be the only person to be assessed. While the CAF accepts the need to involve parents, for example, in an assessment of their child, their views as to the professional practices or services on offer do not form part of the same picture. Similarly, while the professional is directed to consider a young person or their family, analysis of their own practices or indeed the service framework within which they function is absent when clearly these are vital considerations which affect many outcomes in the lives of young people.

That a professional might be required to place within their report the impact upon a child should resources not be available or perhaps provide an analysis of the limits upon their own involvement would certainly be challenging innovations. Obviously, there would be massive financial implications to such a venture and once again it would constitute that delicate balance to be achieved between diversity, cohesion and prosperity which will fuel the movement of the market and thus any professional activity. We can become socialized very quickly into limiting the scope of our opinion and recommendations according to the known and available resources. Should adult professionals and their institutional contexts become part of the broader assessment however, possibly in exposing a lack of provision, a child would of necessity become situated differently – for such a mode of assessment could more realistically reflect that young person's situation where any solutions might be regarded as environmental or social as opposed to individual.

While in the main assessments of young people tend to individualize their situations, nevertheless many childcare professionals are accustomed to assessing the complexity of relationships in young people's lives; for example, with parents as part of care proceedings or with other young people in criminal matters. There is another part of the picture which can often remain invisible, however, for we are not so used to placing under the the microscope the nature of our own relationships with young people. What would assessments look like if the work of professionals was subject not merely to quantitative analysis (for example number of cases, targets achieved and so on), but to a qualitative analysis in respect of our ability to engage and work with the young person in question? This would, of course, go well beyond any current checklist approach.

Now some of those principles traditionally underpinning assessments of young people are based on essentialist models which ignore the impact that an adult professional can have upon a child or which disregard the impact of those testing regimes located at the heart of many practices. Any professional-child relationship can remain hidden behind such a sleight of hand, for professionalism has attempted to present itself as being synonymous with 'objectivity'. However, many would now hold this to be mythical and the invisibility of a researcher or childcare worker is no longer a reasonable claim to make. What is happening when a childcare professional (for example psychologist, social worker or educationist) is with a young person if it is not fundamentally a relationship?

CAN PROFESSIONALS (AFFORD TO) BE HUMAN?

This is no mere facetious enquiry but a genuine attempt to articulate the dilemma. Once again there is a danger that the level of analysis within an individual life remains only at the level of the individual and that often in such cases any broader restrictions or possibilities for action can be hidden from view by professionalized language. The particular boundary between 'human' and 'professional' responsibilities was neatly exposed at one training event when a fellow professional admitted publicly that perhaps the most unforgettable moment of their professional career had been the realization, at an individual human level, of the plight of a particular young person and how she was feeling. The professional in question had broken all the rules at a stroke and to the girl's heartfelt plea, "Nobody loves me!" had replied instinctively 'I do!'

What a moment. Clearly there are good reasons why we should defend both ourselves and the young people with whom we work in a responsible manner. However, what of impulse and sentiment? Which of us will have known all too well the needy young person who is desperately seeking love or affection and which of us has not worked hard to erect and maintain some kind of boundary between ourselves and that child?

'Ben' was one such boy who, following removal from the care of his mother, was clearly feeling sad, lonely and probably bewildered. His feelings were of loss and bereavement and my efforts to maintain physical distance were only just sufficient to prevent an 'unacceptable' gesture from him. Thankfully, I managed to keep this distance until the end of the session, but as we bade our farewells in front of other professionals he seized his moment and gave me a big hug. This is what he had wanted at the outset. My professionalism offered me protection but in the process denied any spontaneous 'joy' in the human exchange.

We train professionals, of course, to avoid vulnerablity in such situations and especially warn against promising anything which is either inappropriate or beyond the capacity to deliver. Given the institutionalized and potentially litigious contexts in which we work, in most respects this stance is absolutely vital and especially when the young person before us is vulnerable to such hopes. However, an acknowledgement here of the human living inside the professional is clear. To what extent, though, can the long-term insistence on a more clinical 'objective' approach destroy our human responses and if this is so, to what extent will such a position ultimately restrict, even disable, our powers of analysis?

Some of my own seminal experiences date back to professional training when my equilibrium was disturbed on two separate occasions and on several counts. Firstly, I was surprised during an observation by the extent to which I found myself identifying with the position of one young boy ('Michael') when working with his psychologist. Secondly, and probably related to this, I was struck by the power imbalance between a professional and another young boy. And lastly, it seemed as though in the respective dyads between professional and child, the adults on these occasions were each somehow oblivious to the intelligence and the sensitive emotional responses of the children involved. The latter seemed to have much keener social antennae, constantly looking and checking for clues as to what was going on, while the adults' attention seemed focused on achieving a particular outcome, for example, the end of a session, the confirmation of a hypothesis or the mere acquisition of data.

It was notable during the course of assessments that both of the young boys we had observed were at times reduced to tears.

Could that have been due to the unsettling presence of this author? This seems possible. Given the nature of their emotional responses though, it also seems likely that each of the boys will have long-retained some kind of memory of the event. The effects of this distress as a training exercise have also been life-lasting for me. I was thus acutely aware, right at the start of my professional career, that whatever the activity or circumstance and whatever position taken by the adult professional, young people will consider themselves during assessment as being 'in-relation-to' that adult. As such, whether we like it or not, when we are with a child we are in a human relationship and our assessment activities form part of that relationship. This critical standpoint holds that whatever the nature of our activity, however innocuous or seemingly 'objective', we are intervening directly in the life of a young person and we must take seriously the impact we make as well as making explicit to ourselves those decisions as to the limits of our availability.

In both these cases a young person was being subjected to psychometric testing and so for some time I was most critical of such work, not least for the underpinning assumptions inherent in such materials, for example the notion of a reductionist 'ability'. However, being required by service practices to conduct tests on occasion with young people I gradually came to realize that such activities do not always cause distress. After many years' experience, while some young people can still become emotional during testing, often their responses are related to feelings of pride as they achieve some success. I cannot pretend that the power imbalance has been overcome and perhaps it could be argued that I have just become more skilful in manipulating these children, nevertheless some children do seem to find such situations rewarding and even enjoyable.

However, whatever transpires between the professional and the child, for good or ill, it still remains a relationship – whether the child wishes to co-operate and engage, remain at a distance or leave the room, which should always be offered as a possibility. Whatever I might prefer, if I am doing my job correctly I should be available to the young person before me in terms of that relationship, however restricted. Once again, the power differential should not be overlooked. Although there will be certain tasks in which I will direct a young person, they should always have a choice – whether to leave or stay, whether to work, or whether to respond (not an option in most educational contexts). Each decision and activity, of course, would resonate emotionally within the context of a purposeful relationship.

ASSESSMENTS AND RELATIONSHIPS

An important principle of practice, therefore, is to recognize that any assessment constitutes a relationship and is potentially an important moment in the life of a young person. This will be a fundamental basis upon which to conduct any assessment. Furthermore it will not be just professional skills at delivering a test for example or skills in uncovering what a young person thinks or wants which will be crucial, but the manner in which we conduct the following:

- how do we speak of the young person (to others)?
- how do we speak with the young person?
- how do we write of the young person (to others)?

Over recent years, there has been an emerging consensus that the childcare professional might need to avoid the traditional objective stance and instead engage. As such 'Particular attention is paid to the skills involved in talking with children, and enabling children to talk in ways that feel safe and take account of the loyalty binds in which they find themselves' (Dowling and Barnes, 2000: 6). Importantly, however, just how do we listen to the young person?

In the incidents encountered above during training, it seemed to me that experienced professionals had ceased to listen to these young people or presumably they would have responded differently to the clearly visible distress and would have been alert to such possibilities, taking steps to avoid or at least alleviate the distress in front of them. However, there have been innumerable occasions in my own practice when I have either been unwilling or unable to sustain a more sensitive engagement. At such moments, one further question thus presents itself. How do we listen to ourselves in professional practice?

In considering training curricula for all those who work with young people, therefore, I would suggest that rather than devising schemes which purport to consider an issue whether in educational, psychological or sociological terms (for example and stereotypically, learning difficulties, 'medicalized' psychopathology or child protection), the five question-themes (p. 8) would demand first and foremost that from the start we place ourselves in relationship to the young person with whom we are working.

Childcare professionals could currently stand accused of erecting barriers against such a demand. Or else we are, at the very least, complicit with the tendency to continually assess children without the resources for adequate follow-up work or specific interventions. So, for example, whereas social workers might in the past have provided some kind of therapeutic services, increasingly work with children seems to be restricted by a requirement for some form of statutory assessment; whilst psychologists grow in number and therapeutic services expand, sometimes the intensity of any programme is restricted to the necessity for 'throughput' and simple outcomes in order to meet corporate targets. Time-limited interventions are generated, for example, by consultation conducted with adults rather than with the child (Wagner, 2000) or brief solution-focused therapy with the child (DeShazer, 1988). Teachers too are subject to a curriculum and government targets in which opportunities for casual and playful interaction with young people are being reduced. As such, quantity is the desired object and quality remains both secondary and elusive.

What remains crucial, however, is not necessarily the activity itself but the availability of the professional as perceived by a young person through the quality of their work of whatever kind, whether assessment or another form of intervention. The relevance of viewing professional work through the lens of relationships has often revealed itself in surprising ways. One of the features of autism, for example, is supposedly the poor social competences possessed by the autistic child. That a determining factor of success with autistic children could be the relationship they are offered by an adult will be known to many families, but this flies in the face of many established professional ideas and positions (see also Billington et al., 2000).

My own casework suggests that, even when assessing a child, there exists the possibility for a relationship which can itself be therapeutic in the broadest sense – which creates the possibility for positive change. For example, many children have become engrossed in the performance of what have been designed primarily as 'tests' and experience has shown that they can begin unexpectedly to play, grow and even luxuriate in such activities. What is happening here?

The welfare and education of young people occupy the minds and activities of thousands of professionals across our current institutions and agencies and there are many models which can help us to undertake the process. Looking beyond nature and nurture as two simplistic polarities, I would suggest that the most useful models here are those in which an individual and their inherently social being are not wrenched apart and that it is the nature of a human relationship, conceived in its totality, which can provide the simple yet crucial point of analysis.

PSYCHODYNAMIC ACCOUNTS

There exists between any human beings a potential space which we can choose to occupy or not. Winnicott (1971) saw the origins of this potential space as deriving originally from the earliest times shared by a mother and her baby and which ultimately leads to the infant's use of what he refers to as 'transitional objects.' Transitional objects permit a point of safe contact between the two which offers possibilities for the development of imagination and intelligence of all kinds, and not just for the infant (for example, a doll, a toy or other artefact). All materials which are utilized in the exchanges between childcare professionals and their child clients also possess this potential to be used as a transitional object, as a means of negotiating a relationship and playing with ideas and feelings safely. Assessments which utilize a range of professional artefacts, even those designed as 'tests', can still allow us to enjoin in that most fundamental and rewarding of human social exchanges – the sharing of communication and tool-use (Vygotsky, 1986). As such assessments are interventions, but they are also human relationships.

While Winnicott concentrated on mother-baby interactions, Piontelli (1992) suggests that such interactive possibilities occur even earlier and helps us to conceptualize that the foetus too will develop in relation to their own particular environmental context. Thinking of our work in terms of human relationships therefore (how else could they be conceived?) would affect the kind of work we conduct. What would the curriculum begin to look like if the various professional training courses were organized primarily to develop the abilities of trainees to conduct (ethical) relationships with their child clients?

Obviously there are existing models of practice which have espoused such principles. For example, a search for a Rogerian (1951) 'empathy' or 'unconditional positive regard' would seem a useful if somewhat incomplete and perhaps impossible start, for there are some young people with whom I have worked where I have found such states difficult to sustain. For example, during one of my home visits the sudden violence of a young man who sought to assault his mother was beyond any simple manipulation or massaging of human sensibilities.

As I have hinted at previously, however, there are sophisticated models which can guide us through the complexities of interpersonal relationships. For example, the *object-relations school* in psychology encourages a knowledge of projection, transference and counter-transference as being crucial to an understanding of professional-child relationships, whether during assessment, in representation or by more overt intervention. One therapist known to me created a wonderful scenario for exploration of these issues which, by focusing on the functions of closeness and distance in human relationships, helped to reveal vital concepts in work with young people (Turton, M., c1997).

Transference

'For many authors the notion has taken on a very broad extension, even coming to connote all the phenomena which constitute the patient's relationship with the psychoanalyst ... Freud looks upon transference ... as just a particular instance of displacement of affect from one idea to another...'. (Laplanche and Pontalis, 1973: 455–62)

Counter-transference

'a result of the patient's influence on [the physician's] unconscious feelings ... treatment come more and more to be understood as a relationship'. (Laplanche and Pontalis, 1973: 92–3)

The client was placed in an imaginary tennis match on one side of the net, and the other person (family member, client or whoever) on the other side. The game would start and each person would have some control over the shots they made. The weight of the shot, its direction or speed for example could be controlled and the receiver would have to return the shot accordingly, either in a manner which sustained the rally (interaction) or sought to curtail it, perhaps by hitting a winner. Both players could adjust their positions, sometimes trading ground shots from the back of the court, sometimes coming up to the net for a quick-fire exchange. However, some shots would be impossible to return whether received or delivered.

The concept of closeness and distance (see also Wilkinson, 1993: 126) would seem a useful analogy for our work with young people and its potential is that it might never allow our perception of a young person to evolve outside of the context of a knowledge and relationship that exist on the court. It does also, however, create a useful point of analysis since clearly a move by either player to the other side of the net would constitute a transgression in respect of the rules of the game between professional and child. As such any assessment work we conduct, conceptualized as a relationship, would permit both parties to operate safely in a process of hypothesis-formation which has the potential to sustain, encourage and develop the length of the rallies and would therefore encourage the participation of the young client: 'Hypothesis formation rather than testing was therefore and still is largely my aim' (Piontelli, 1992: 8).

In such interactionist models pathology can be detached from the child and even disappear. It was just the case at one point during my professional training when I was being exhorted to work with 'Michael', who had multiple and profound disabilities. It was not clear to me the extent to which he would perceive my actions as an intrusion upon his side of the net and this needed to be tested. How could this be done, however, without due sensitivity to the complexities of human feeling within the terms of a relationship for which both participants might be ill-prepared? Such caution perhaps illuminates those contexts more commonly experienced by young people and thus demands of us interventions which are designed with the individual in mind.

FUTURE WORK

I offer the following as resources upon which good practice with children can be based:

In the social domain, knowledge and power are inextricably interrelated.' (White and Epston, 1990: viii)

School experiences are likely to be of great importance. Attention and warmth shown by the teachers are key factors. (Dowling and Barnes, 2000: 25)

Our everyday social interactions can be often taken for granted. Paradoxically, their significance may be overlooked because they are so important, so fundamental ... attention to others can result in an illusion that we do not exist and cannot be seen in our work, either by ourselves or by others. (Billington, 1995: 36)

More than this, however, whether or not we choose to view our assessments of young people as occurring within the context of social relationships we cannot escape the fact that whatever our assessment activity we are intervening in their lives. An assessment, therefore, is itself an intervention. As such, it is our responsibility to remain capable of attending ethically to our side of the human relationship by being sensitive to the effects and consequences of our interventions.

FURTHER READING

Dowling, E. and Barnes, G. G. (2000) *Working with Children and Parents through Separation and Divorce.* Basingstoke: Palgrave Macmillan.
Vygotsky, L. S. (1986) *Thought and Language.* Cambridge, MA: Harvard University Press.

Wilkinson, I. (1993) *Child and Family Assessment: Clinical guide for Practitioners*. London: Routledge.

Winnicott, D. W. (1971) *Playing and Reality*. London: Tavistock.

Winnicott, D. W. (1977) *The Piggle: An account of the psychoanalytic treatment of a little girl*. London: Penguin.

Reflexive Activity

Choose a young person with whom you are to meet as part of your professional work. Record the session in some way and analyse according to the principles of closeness and distance. Ask the young person for their views on your relationship. Were some young people excluded from your consideration? If so, what factors restricted your choice? (Be careful to seek appropriate approvals beforehand from the young person and relevant adults.)

5 REPRESENTING CHILDREN AND YOUNG PEOPLE IN ASSESSMENTS

> Adam's disability was not just visible in the sense that the world was a neutral medium for what he could not do, but that the world was precisely organized for making his disability apparent, that he was the negative achievement of a school system that insisted that everyone do better than everyone else.
>
> (Hood et al., 1980, in McDermott, 1993: 273)

Experiencing a childhood in 1950s Britain can now be remembered in a warm glow; as fond memories evoked in occasional reruns of radio and television programmes of the day. The sun seemed to shine and good order would prevail, protected as we were by Robin Hood, Roy Rogers and even George Dixon.

In school, the values inculcated were woven seamlessly with those of another institution – the Church – and for many of us Sunday Schools were part of how life was lived. The remembrance of a safe existence with father at work for long hours and mother waiting for us with a hot meal ready to put on the table when we got home can be hard to resist. Even the map of the world was reassuring, with pink dominating the globe. But was it really ever just like this? Was Harold Macmillan right when he pronounced 'you've never had it so good'? Well, no doubt this could have been true for some. For others the 1950s would be remembered as dreary and drab.

If I think back carefully enough though I too can play with memory. From an early age we had an understanding that around one corner of the street from where we lived there were wealthy people living in large houses, while just around the other corner there were streets in which 'poor' people lived, all of us in close proximity. Children from the wealthy homes didn't seem to attend my school; children from poor houses, while attending my school, were somehow 'different'. For example, the clothes they wore, their smell and the way in which, year after year, they didn't contribute so generously to worthy charities (in my case, the annual 'Good Shepherd' collection for poor black children). Then I remember my confusion as the barefoot African boy who I had been saving from starvation suddenly turned up in class and sat right next to me, albeit now shoeclad. It was a long time before I realized that life did not stand still.

OF HISTORY, MEMORY AND THE MAKING OF KNOWLEDGE

A dominant theme running through my childhood was the Second World War and the defeat of Hitler – always a source of national, local and familial pride – but above all there was play. While it seemed to me then that evil had been overcome for all time, we know of course that before too long war was eventually followed by civil unrest, whether in protest against employment conditions, nuclear weapons, or race riots in London and Alabama. Britain also suffered a national humiliation at Suez (1956). Clearly, I was either protected from such realities or else they were singularly irrelevant to me at the time.

Such reflections, of course, are quite useful in reminding us that we can each have different memories of the same points in history and that each individual will possess remembrances of childhood with their own unique qualities. This is not to say that all memory is reconstructed in such a way as to deny the existence of a shared reality, but in respect of issues to be discussed it is sufficient to reiterate that the children with whom we work will have different priorities and interests and that these might change over time.

Since those sunny days and cocoa-fuelled nights of my own childhood there have been wars too numerous to mention, fuel crises, the collapse of the Soviet bloc and, of course, Margaret Thatcher and Tony Blair. More recently, capitalism has seemed to become reinvigorated by the growth of internet technology and new economies in the Far East; even the British economy has revived from a previously terminal decline. Somehow though there still seem to be those 'other' children; the poor, for whom money is scarce, whose clothes are cheap and whose homes are dirty. These children stubbornly resist all attempts to remove them from government statistics – be they economic, educational or health-based.

The discomfort I can feel now in professional work when entering an alien neighbourhood or visiting a threadbare home is one I am prepared to tolerate (in part, for financial gain) but to what extent does my own relative privilege underpin professional judgments about those homes, the children therein and their experiences and memories?

We know that life can be very different according to who you are and where and when you are living. So a cosy remembrance of my mother always at home as a bedrock not just for the family but for life itself now sits uneasily alongside questions about other kinds of life she might have lived or what her life meant to her. Feminism, of course, provides a critique against which to see such lives but any obvious politicized dogma somehow seems incongruous with who she was or at least my memory of her. And yet she was precisely that example of a woman who could have lived a different life at a different time.

POLITICAL CRITIQUE OR SOCIAL SCIENTIFIC THEORY?

While the particularity of her life could be thought of in political, economic, sociological or psychological terms, perhaps today Attachment would provide an easier theoretical perspective with which to view my mother's life or rather to view my life in relation to hers (Ainsworth et al., 1978; Belsky, 1999). Certainly the bonds that existed between her and myself and my siblings as children have lasted our lifetimes and beyond hers, but then these are my memories and constructions. It is interesting though that once again Attachment as a theoretical/practitioner resource emerged at just that particular moment in history.

We each have our own memories and conceive of our own identities in relation to others and the Internal Working Model of attachment theorists (Bowlby, 1988) provides theoretical sustenance at this point. The importance of 'position', however, is not merely a post-modern concept, but one which is essential if we are to understand not only the children we meet but also the ways in which we choose to portray them in our professional work. The apparent erosion of old values and certainties has been reflected in and perhaps hastened by changes in economic and indeed intellectual production. During the last decade new technologies have allowed many to engage with the prospect of alternative 'realities' while the possibility of leading multiple lives, amassing a range of hitherto undreamt of experiences, has been extended to many as part of the capitalist project of expanding choice.

Internal Working Model

'Attachment theory holds that, within close relationships, young children acquire mental representations, or internal working models, of their own worthiness based on other people's availability and their ability to provide care and protection'. (Ainsworth et al., 1978, in D. Howe et al., 1999: 21)

Within the world of academia, for some time the only home of knowledge, new theories emerged which fuelled change – feminism has gone hand-in-hand with structuralism, post-structuralism and post-modernism as a means of challenging existing power bases. Others might counter that it is through such analyses that the chosen targets of such movements have been able to reconstitute and restrict the extent of any reform. While a critique of these movements is not within the remit of this book, the proponents of the various 'isms' have, together with the phenomenon of the internet, contributed to intellectual and economic change not only in respect of our access to knowledge, but in our whole approach to what we consider knowledge and expertise. What can be known and who knows it can no longer be taken for granted and this change is having an impact on our lives and upon the institutions which have for decades acted as part of the framework of our civilization – the web of governmentality.

As practitioners we can now meet clients who have already surfed the internet to access knowledge about a whole range of issues – whether legal rights, financial obligations, or in relation to their children, specific psychopathologies or diagnoses. How easy it is to access knowledge now, real knowledge at your fingertips, 'truth' which can provide reassurance when certainty has elsewhere been abandoned and when all around is confusing. How difficult it is becoming then to prepare professionals to acquire knowledge when that knowledge is not only available elsewhere and in vast quantities, but is also changing fast.

More than this, however, for not only is knowledge changing fast but it can seem to differ according to the position of the participants. How then and upon what knowledge bases do professionals construct their work with children and young people?

THEORETICAL PREFERENCES

I trained as a psychologist when psychodynamic approaches had become unfashionable, derided as they were for being unscientific, and at a time when behavioural approaches were being heralded as a panacea for whole-scale application across a range of client issues, from trauma to reading problems to a 'cure' for autism. I quickly became just one of the many who, having been drawn to the study of psychology by its promise to address profound professional human questions, was to be disappointed by its strategic ideological embrace of the positivist tradition. As a result psychology has consistently struggled to deal with the truly social nature of human beings and the complexity of the relationship with our clients within professional practices has often evaded analysis. Occasionally our explanations of what it is to be human have seemed incomprehensible (or perhaps that is the unwitting purpose).

Its potential as a means of gaining understanding of the human condition, however, has not been extinguished and there are many who in their daily practice have persisted in trying to find ways of working which could resist the tendency to create elisions where there should be consideration of meaning, understanding or the experience of social exchange. In addition, there have been individuals who have inspired in future generations an urge to maintain a basis for work with people on the principles of social justice, emancipation and ethical practice; William James, Lev Vygotsky and more recently Jerome Bruner and Noamh Chomsky, but also others too numerous to mention, have provided inspirational models for such work. In particular, it has been young people themselves who have, through their own unique qualities, demanded that I assume my responsibilities. Certainly, keeping in mind such principles of justice and emancipation has frequently been difficult and discomfiting and has seemed at times to be leading me to the edges of professional marginalization, perhaps analogous to the marginalization of those children with whom we work.

But then why should 'Paul' or 'Sammy' not be able to live with their mother for example, if that is what they want (Chapter 2)? Their wishes seemed quite reasonable especially when all the various childcare agencies had flooded into their respective lives because of poverty, it could be argued, rather than on account of any underlying psychological causes; simply economic, educational or communal reasons. For the threads of the communities in which those boys lived were almost bare; the resources woefully thin. Rehabilitation can become unthinkable in such cases and yet we can still base practice on the understanding that we will work to achieve what is in the 'best interests' of the child. In day-to-day practice of course there is a demand for certainty and clarity in thought and delivery of service, not to mention the general expectation that we have access to special forms of knowledge. Childcare workers should be employed because of a knowledge and expertise about children, not for their acumen as financial consultants or political commentators.

The situations which present themselves, however, can be messy and can throw up just as many questions as answers. Such tendencies on my part (in providing questions when answers were sought) caused a good friend and colleague to remark once that I seemed to be "better with questions than with answers". This has sometimes seemed akin to an acknowledgement of incompetence, but I clung to my friend's analysis by finding theories which supported not a lack of clarity but a mode of critical analysis which could support and develop a more informed practice.

A search began for research, theories and practices which were based not on obvious or specific knowledge but upon principles of practice which juxtapose the simple and the complex, the superficial and the profound. While difficult, such principles have always seemed more suited to a human science in practice. Piontelli's (1992) notion of 'hypothesis formation rather than testing' once again seems to capture an important principle of practice, while Bion's complex (1962) theory of learning has always seemed to resonate (he recommends the avoidance of a too-early closure on acceptance of knowledge as 'fact' in order to allow a more active process of learning and knowing to develop).

In this chapter, therefore, I will provide glimpses of ideas which have become foundations for work with children although the chosen starting point might not appear at first sight to be easily absorbed into professional work.

LANGUAGE AND THE SOCIAL

During the twentieth century there was a 'turn to language' as a site for intellectual endeavour across a wide range of disciplines, from philosophy (Wittgenstein, 1953) to communication sciences (Chomsky, 1986) and psychology (Vygotsky, 1978, 1986). There are clearly many others who could be cited as making massive contributions to the way in which we investigate and build a knowledge of our species. However, just as some of the ideas commonly associated with Freud or Darwin have left the academy to invade popular culture and knowledge (for example, 'the unconscious' or 'survival of the fittest' – which was actually a term coined by Spencer), the idea now that words might not always mean exactly what they say has become an accepted wisdom which has similarly left the academy. In this respect, it is impossible to deny the contribution of Derrida (1978), Foucault (1972) and Lacan (1977). At the same time, while some professionals would consider such critiques as providing helpful explanations for contemporary cultural confusions, others might view them as fuelling the fires of social destruction.

Vygotsky, of course, considered the origins of language to be the catalyst for thought itself and as such that it distinguishes us from all other creatures on the planet. Not only this, for while the development of language could be seen as an individualized (biological) phenomenon, Vygotsky suggested that the fusion between language and thinking was embedded first of all in the infant's relation to the social world. He further suggested that the infant would come to use language and thinking as a means of internal communication, of communicating with oneself only as a consequence of an earlier primary connection with that social world.

Unknown to Vygotsky, Hanna Segal (1986), working from what was seemingly a very different knowledge base (psychoanalysis), was examining just that very phenomenon – our ability to communicate with ourselves, as it were, internally and through symbolic means. Yet always, the *object-relations* base of her work while being concerned with the individual was by its very definition located in social interactions which provided the setting, context and material for the individual life.

Object Relations

'is the entire complex outcome of a particular organization of the personality, of an apprehension of objects that is to some extent or other phantasied, and of certain special types of defence'. (Laplanche and Pontalis, 1973: 277–81)

There are many other examples of late twentieth century psychologists whose work has been comfortably placed within a humanist, social framework of ideas about human development and functioning, for example Erikson ([1951] 1995), Bruner (1986, Bruner and Haste, 1990) and Margaret Donaldson (1978). In psychoanalysis Klein ([1957] 1988), Winnicott (1971), Bion (1962, 1970), and more recently Peter Hobson (2002) have similarly rooted the psychology of early development in undeniably social terms (that is, in human relationships). It is to these works that practitioners need to look if we are to understand more of any individual child working with us, not as an isolated phenomenon sat separately across the table from us but as posited within the professional-child dyad – which in turn must be seen as nothing other than a relationship.

PROFESSIONAL PRACTICE AS RELATIONSHIPS

In any human exchange we can attempt to deny the importance of another but whatever the response, whether positive or negative, what is undeniable is that there is a relationship. When a professional works with a child we are not merely providing an analysis or imparting knowledge, we are 'in relation-to'. More than this, and whatever trajectory the relationship takes, we will be 'in-relation-to' the other which posits us not only in the professional-child dyad, but in a bigger world of others with whom we are also 'in-relation-to'. This dilemma returns us to the original meeting-place between psychology and sociology and the questions which propelled the works of Galton (1869, 1883), Spencer (1876, 1861, 1900) and James (1902).

Piaget (1936) understood such interactive possibilities in the world of the infant in concepts such as 'object-permanence'. However, while the individual is placed in a wider context of otherness, in Piaget's work it is only the child who is perceived as the agent while that otherness can tend to be reduced to the status of an inhuman 'object'.

Prior to that there had been a headlong plunge into that world in which the child operates as an island, an isolated and trapped entity with fixed and unchangeable characteristics and intelligences, impervious to the environmental and social contexts. IQ and 'g' were both ill-fated attempts to lock young people into an unyielding life course that, once embarked upon, would allow no deviation or escape (Spearman, 1904; Binet and Simon, 1905). Such notions have, of course, proved to be virulent and long-lasting despite their vulnerability to scientific critique and they continue to support narrow, within-child approaches. Indeed, it is possible now to see the extent to which all services for children and young people still invoke 'ability' as a decisive arbiter of professional practice.

It is little wonder that psychodynamic ideas before and after the Second World War should prove popular since the individualized model often being presented was at least more recognizable in its interactive potentials, for example in object relations psychology (Klein, 1932, 1957) and personal construct psychology (Kelly, 1955), transactional analysis (Foulkes, 1964) or group work (Lewin, 1948; Bion, 1961). The broader context for living in 1940s Britain, however, seemed to leave an indelible mark on all those who knew of the war and while the experiences were clearly individual, accounts of that era are so intrinsically social in quality that they tend to overwhelm any contradictory representations of the individual which are removed from that context.

Attachment theory, of course, should by its very definition be the most innately social of all concepts, focusing at the outset on the phenomenon of the mother-child bond. However, this theory has also at times developed and propagated effectively in ways which deny the primacy of social or qualitative aspects of human exchange and instead provide a model dependent on biological or behavioural explanations at the expense of others (for example psychodynamic, sociological or political analyses).

Foulkes (1964), Lewin (1948), Perls et al. (1951) and Kelly (1955), however, all attempted to provide psychological models which acknowledged the centrality of the social aspect of our being and in the works of Winnicott we also see the ultimate fruition of a process of theory development in which imagination, play and human 'potential' are the focus rather than subsidiary lines of inquiry (see for example *Playing and Reality*, 1971). Winnicott views that first relationship between infant and mother as a 'potential space' in which both can explore that relationship freely – a model which suggests that each locates the other, experiences the feeling and interprets the feeling-state of the other in a reciprocal and social process.

Winnicott's placement of the mother and child in a world of otherwise inanimate objects allows these to be utilitarian in a rather Vygotskyan reverie, as supports for what remains an essentially human drama of players and tool-users. While the social conditions prevailing in post-war Britain encouraged a climate in which the infant would be seen primarily as being 'in-relation-to' the mother these circumstances have changed, however, and fathers as well as other family members are now considered as attachment figures.

I well remember the birth of my third child and after a physically exhausting delivery for mother and baby, and an immediate clean-up and cuddle, I was then left to hold the baby for a while. He cooed and searched with all his senses but each time I put him in the cot he started to cry. I would pick him up and he would stop. We then repeated this pattern as alternatively he lay contented in my arms and cried in protest at my disappearance (or unavailability) as I put him down.

Clearly, there can be all kinds of readings of this sequence of events and we can each make our preferred theoretical choice. Essentialists can justifiably lay claim to the instinct of the newborn to demand and ensure its needs for survival are met. Social interactionists meanwhile can point to the psychodynamic notion that from the outset the baby's interactions reveal not only a desired survival but desire itself; which is just one of the qualities in the multiplicity of activities and feelings that he or she will absorb and come to know as the social. That there are links between our physical and sensory experience is increasingly compelling, while what could be described as our cognitive or emotional worlds, however, would seem to depend on the presence or development of a symbolic life (Segal, 1986; Billington, 2000a; Hobson, 2002) but this anticipates themes explored in Chapters 6 and 8.

FIVE QUESTION–THEMES

Returning to those five questions then – how do we speak of the young person (to others)?; how do we speak with the young person?; how do we write of the young person (to others)?; how do we listen to the young person?; how do we listen to ourselves? These are designed to reveal that there are choices to be made as to whether to reveal or to omit aspects of being in the words we use and in the relationships in which we are engaged when working with children. These are the sites for the continual dilemmas that present themselves in professional work with all young people.

Clearly, words are not the same as experience and in those moments of physical togetherness with my son feelings arose which are beyond this author's powers of accurate description. I was not consciously thinking as a psychologist, but Winnicott's theory of potential space to which both adult and infant direct attention is an enduring concept which seems to provide a theoretical explanation applicable to all human relationships. A baby's desire for survival is not an isolated desire but part of social exchange. Any purely physical needs were being accompanied by a human response which offered not merely physical comfort but more – and increasingly the psychological possibilities within such an interaction have become recognized. Perhaps derivatives of such possibilities lie not just between a parent and their infant child, however, but between us as professionals and the young people with whom we work.

While the stages of development envisaged by Piaget (1936) are still helpful (a principle adopted not just by developmental psychology but throughout the social sciences), more and more it is becoming obvious that the new-born baby has a range of potentials which become activated during the earliest social exchanges, in ways hitherto unsuspected. These interactions are not just mere sensory responses but develop into spontaneity, predictability and capacity for change (or not), and always there are those feelings which are an integral part of the sensory experience. Peter Hobson's (2002) work graphically illustrates this link, often ignored, between our sensory and emotional worlds which is learned through interaction with the world of objects and people.

Bion (1962, 1970), of course, had previously begun to articulate this connectivity, which is far from saying that an infant becomes the person with whom they are interacting. However, there are choices that can be made in respect of which aspects of the other person might be utilized and what might be rejected. The concepts of transference, counter-transference, projection and projective identification, while obviously imperfect continue to provide a coherent theoretical template for understanding something of this to-and-fro process of interaction between infants and their parents.

Now clearly, any words used in this particular account remain just that – words. There are limits to their powers of explanation; there are similar limits, therefore, to their ability to convey either my experience or that of my son. There is a fissure between experience and any explanations of that experience and Lacan's (1977) model of discourse analysis provides a helpful theoretical resource at this point for making clear that all our accounts will be problematic in their claims to truth. This is not the same as saying that there is no absolute truth. Just that it cannot easily be known.

To Lacan, the language we use will be subject to possible interpretations even at the moment of utterance; not only on account of the many possibilities within us, but also on account of the experiences brought to the words by a reader or listener. Lacan's distinction between the 'signifier' (the concrete life of the word itself) and the 'signified' (those possible meanings that live inside and beyond the word) suggests that while our language develops as part of the web of feeling and thinking, all cannot be captured within the words themselves (see also Hollway, 1989; Billington, 1995, 2000a).

In our professional lives, however, we often enter into a pretence that all can be contained in the words, for example in a diagnosis, definition or explanation. We need to believe that we are understanding what is being said not only in order that we can trust whoever our social partner is at the time, but also in order that we may feel that our own subsequent actions are based on a sound knowledge and understanding. That we might not always be able to trust words clearly has implications for our professional lives.

Vygotsky's earlier thesis was that psychology had done little to tackle the thorny problem of 'word meaning' and there have been many others who remain necessarily cautious on account of this very issue (Segal, 1986; Shotter, 1990; Mannoni, 1999). This should not paralyze us into believing that nothing can be known because clearly things are known, but it is surely incumbent on practitioners to appreciate the following three distinctions:

- between the diagnosis and the child;
- between a knowledge of children generally and our interpretations of the child before us;
- between any descriptions of the child we construct and the descriptions that the child might potentially construct for themselves.

There is little wonder that confusion abounds in the aftermath of a tragic case such as Victoria Climbie, for the sheer volume of the issues is almost beyond rational analysis. But that confusion only becomes overwhelming if we expect too much of words for while the words before us might strive towards categorical closure, the possible theoretical choices before us in our lives appear to be expanding exponentially. Lacan implied that not only were human beings expert communicators but we were also expert in the field of 'miscommunication' (Lacan, 1977; Hollway, 1989). Surely we have known too long of the gaps that occur between a diagnosis, supposedly factual knowledge and an understanding of the experience of the young person in question.

LUKE

'Luke' did not know that school staff were wondering whether he was 'Asperger's'. Even if he did, what could it mean to him? Certainly, thoughts and questions on the part of the teachers seemed perfectly reasonable. Here they had a boy of good intelligence, who was a little isolated and a tad unusual both in his behaviours and in his style of social communication. He seemed to me, however, to be an articulate, sensible and sensitive boy, a young person any of us would be proud to name as our son (although this representation was never to constitute part of my assessment or intervention).

At the same time, he did not seem to be achieving academically in the way that he should and he often seemed either vague or somehow inaccessible. He could on occasion do something out of the ordinary or which seemed bizarre, such as running out of school yet not knowing his way home (although at secondary level). Those teachers were not aware, however, that Luke was in the middle of a bitter custody battle.

Unknown to school staff, over the years a story had been constructed in Luke's family which hinged on this: that his mother was incompetent. Admittedly his mother had been young when she gave birth to Luke and had undoubtedly found it difficult always to act in ways which placed his needs as paramount. For example, she seemed to want an active social life and she had on occasion left him with a babysitter, who was subsequently alleged to have been unsuitable. In retrospect it could be said that she was struggling to cope with some long-standing family issues but she had always held on to him and had cared for him as best she could. At one point, in order not to lose Luke completely, she had enlisted the support of a close family member. Unfortunately the contribution of this family member ('Peter') was so overpowering that eventually Luke became the subject of an emotional tug-of-war whereby the conflict developed to such an extent that Peter took steps to wrest control of Luke from his mother through the court system.

Now there were many other issues in this case which could each lay claim to being important in the family's history and relationships between family members. During assessment it became clear that Luke would have many different stories to choose from and subsequently upon which my opinion could be based. Those involving his mother, Peter and several other significant family members presented in very diverse ways and understanding them demanded as much of me as Luke, who was simultaneously the focus of intense interest from each family member. But being subjected to such scrutiny meant that Luke's voice could barely be heard amongst this cacophony of adults, family and professionals.

I had been instructed only to assess Luke and his sister and so it was clearly vital to access his view. It must be said that children (as with adults) can become confused not only by the voices around them, but by attempting to piece together a history of their own lives, when various factions can each deliver such very different and vivid versions, all forcefully expressed. Luke seemed not only confused but almost overwhelmed, in particular by the strength of the two principal adult positions as reflected in their views and feelings. To these he was almost constantly subjected.

Luke's good intelligence suggested that, intellectually or cognitively, he was perfectly able to provide an account of his own but his very survival was in the hands of two protagonists who were locked in a seemingly mortal combat. Although he never admitted to it, I hypothesized that he was scared. In particular, I hypothesized that he was scared lest he become annihilated in a battle between the two foes; which was no idle fantasy for during assessment the full effects of the situation on him were becoming clear, not just in his efforts to be kind to each party but in the tears rolling silently down his cheeks as he spoke with me.

But just as my own new-born babe had desired to luxuriate in my arms, Luke too seemed to want to rest secure in his family. What was his reward though since any feelings of love that either his mother or Peter had for him were penetrated by hatred of one another? He might well have been hearing these words but he was perhaps understanding only too well the feelings that lay inside and beyond, the harsh invective they directed at each other. Luke never said any of this. These are purely my interpretations.

Surely such interpretations can be dangerous? They can be, for they constitute professional opinion that is based not just on a factual knowledge of an individual's circumstances and possible diagnosis but one which endeavours to remain rooted in a social world of qualities, experience and dilemmas (Billig et al., 1988). What to do then, when Luke declared that he wanted to live apart from his mother? In my opinion he chose to utilize the discourse that his mother was incompetent. Again, only in my opinion, he both feared Peter and *for* Peter even more and knew the potential consequences were he not to comply with his wishes.

I shall reiterate here that in working with children we need to construct our practices upon interactionist models which place, as central, the views of the young person. However, this presupposes that an individual child is any better than an adult in being able to arrive at an all-embracing or unproblematic conclusion at such times. How do we listen to that young person, therefore, and which theories can help us to achieve the necessary state of awareness and help us to track our way through the density of information with which we are confronted?

A young person who is subject to such internecine family warfare is likely to be confused emotionally and psychologically. At one point during individual assessment, however, it became clear the extent to which Luke had never before had the opportunity or space to think about his family in conditions of safety. Presumably when with one family member he had become accustomed to sharing a particular view of the absent one which allowed him to survive when in their company and vice versa. He had thus developed his own different stories in a manner which allowed him to survive.

The chronology of events in the family was still unclear to me, however, and when I suggested that we do a little work on this in order to help my understanding Luke agreed. At first he performed the Bene-Anthony Family Relations Test with me (Bene and Anthony, 1957). This is in many respects an unacceptably dated instrument and like all such tests is limited in its claims to truth. However, it does explicitly rely on the interpretation of the psychologist which can arise only from an understanding that there is a relationship between the child, the professional and the materials present in their transitional space.

Luke's manner of engagement was such that we continued the work beyond the confines of the test itself. He released his intelligence and while I was aware that he would at some point have to leave the safe conditions of the session, we proceeded to create a map of family members in which he was able to articulate all sorts of ideas, feelings and questions. This was explicitly an assessment but I would suggest again that assessment *is* intervention and as such due care had to be shown in allowing Luke to leave the room with defences intact, especially since I hypothesized that he had for years been painstakingly constructing them.

I suppose from my point of view an abiding memory of Luke is of a boy intently looking at the scene he had constructed in front of him, the figures representing individual family members and, as he began playing with ideas, remembering the ways in which he began to articulate questions about his family and his place within it. While Luke had learned to speak in a particular voice which allowed him to survive outside the room, he was now beginning to experiment with finding other voices which had hitherto been prohibited.

While these other voices might still be dangerous for him, the emancipatory principle was that he might be provided with the space and the resources with which he could more safely arrive at a voice of his own choice. As a professional I had made my own choice – to listen, to represent and thus to intervene in the life of a young person. The assessment was an intervention. It was above all a very special kind of relationship.

Reflexive Activity

Think of a child with whom you have worked and who has some kind of diagnosis. Select a few words which might best describe the qualities possessed by the child. Do your chosen words differ from conventional diagnostic definitions? Also, how might your descriptions be distinguished from those the young person might choose for themselves? (How much) do any differences of linguistic representation matter? What are the implications for the particular child you have in mind?

---

6 CHILDREN FEELING, THINKING AND LEARNING

Feeling [is] an integral part of reason ... the lowly orders of our organism are in the loop of high reason. (Damasio, 1994: xii, xv)

It has been suggested in earlier chapters that in work with young people a consensus of opinion between all participants (for example, young person, parent, social worker, teacher, medic, psychologist) can be far from easy to achieve. Not least one of the causes for this is that some of the theoretical underpinnings of professional practices can be markedly different. Now it is not being suggested here that any such differences of opinion are necessarily a bad thing, for on the contrary such differences may be a strength not only in respect of any science, but also politically and socially in a cycle of challenge, reappraisal and reinvigoration.

Some of the disparities between adult accounts, therefore, are the product of a division of labour between theories of human development and functioning that are embedded in training curricula across the different professions. There could be some 'rationalization' (which is an awful term borrowed from economics); indeed achieving structural change according to economic forces could well be implicit within the UK government's current plans for reshaping the nature of the children's workforce. However, any rationalization of the children's workforce which simplistically places as central individual models of psychopathology at the expense of social or political critiques would not be in the best interests of young people generally, since once again it would leave the broader social conditions unscrutinized, unpoliticized and unchanged.

Knowledge is rarely static and can be subject to alteration, although this is not a case for endless relativism. The contemporary fashion for narrative methods, indeed autobiography in social science research, is one example of a phenomenon in which there is a clash between, on the one hand, individualized narratives of experience and on the other, the pathologizing narratives of empirical science. This context is providing not only a challenge for practitioners but a potential site for the construction of new children's services. There is another conflict, however, which is developing within these scientific investigations and has implications for practice and ultimately for our young clients. For there are theories emerging now which challenge the assumption that the processes of human feelings and thinking are necessarily separate and occurring in isolated mental domains.

Interestingly, while initially apparently born of an intrinsically medical model of psycho-pathology, some recent developments in neuroscience seem to be pointing the way to a potential synthesis with philosophical notions of mind and consciousness. These developments suggest links between our thinking and our feeling which challenge a long-established professionalized division of labour between our cognitive and affective lives. Such developments would, of course, also seem to support those professional approaches which give credence to non-professional accounts of lived experiences as a legitimate source of knowledge. How will children's services respond to those new conceptual possibilities in practice?

A HISTORY OF THINKING AND FEELING

Those big questions from the nineteenth century upon which psychology and sociology were founded will have attracted many of us to the 'caring professions' in the first place; many of these questions, of course, are still largely unanswered. The phrenology of the early nineteenth century marked a clear stage in the development of the discipline of psychology and while most of its conclusions were soon to be dismissed, the principle behind it – the modular structure of the brain – was predictive of discoveries made long after and in recent times. What is now being suggested in contemporary neuroscience, however, is the 'inter-connectedness' of the ways in which this modular structure of the brain actually operates.

In a BBC Radio 3 broadcast a few years ago, Jonathan Bate, erstwhile Professor of English Literature at the University of Liverpool, hosted a programme which involved, amongst others, Peter Hobson (Professor of Child Psychiatry at the Tavistock Clinic) and Susan Greenfield (Professor of Neurophysiology at the University of Oxford). The subject matter of the programme concerned the links and similarities between current research in neuroscience and ideas about the creative and imaginative work of artists, writers and musicians. That our cognitive and emotional lives are disconnected was an idea challenged in a fundamental way.

> For neuroscientists such as Susan Greenfield, connectivity is how we get from brain to mind ... perhaps the imagination is the very principle of connection that [for her] marks the distinction between brain and mind. (Bate, 2003: 9, 11)

In Greenfield's account of severe damage to the prefrontal cortex of one Phineas Gage, she explained how different areas of the brain can be wiped out but 'still leave a whole range of capacities fully intact' (Bate, 2003: 8). However in his accounts of Gage another neuroscientist, Antonio Damasio, found that 'the damage to Gage's prefrontal cortex simultaneously altered both his powers of reasoning and his emotional behaviour' (Bate, 2003: 8–9). Could it be then that there is an emerging consensus between science and art which 'calls into question a long-held belief, going back to Descartes and beyond, that the rational mind and the bodily emotions operate in "altogether separate spheres"'? (Bate, 2003: 9).

Western science has been constructed largely upon Descartes' premise of 'I think, therefore, I am' (Descartes, 1637) in which there not only appears a schism between mind and body, but also a superiority and primacy of the mind linked to a certain kind of thinking. This premise has been hugely influential not only in the development of a particular kind of science, but also in the ways we have come to think psychologically when working with children.

I would argue the need to re-evaluate the usefulness of a simplistic division of labour which prevents discursive contact between branches of knowledge-making, and indeed it may be that seemingly hitherto discrete and totally separate forms of human activity and intellectual pursuit will now have much to gain from reconnecting again. While the work of practitioners in social services has placed as central the emotional well-being of their (child) clients, education services have traditionally been constructed upon a particular mechanistic idea about our mental 'cognitive' lives.

THE MIND IN THE MACHINE (WITH APOLOGIES TO GILBERT RYLE, 1949)

For some psychologists the mind was viewed as a machine in which there were predictable routes and stable categories; one such entity, of course, was the concept of intelligence. During the last one hundred years or so, the focus on an individual's intelligence often came to be considered in practice as stable, immovable and even immune to environmental circumstances. While Binet would not have foreseen the outcomes of his endeavours, the widespread adoption of testing regimes based only on narrow concepts of human cognition has underpinned the training of many psychologists and educationists, obscuring the profound questions and issues which underpinned the work of early pioneers in the social sciences (perhaps most noteworthy here are Herbert Spencer and William James). Interestingly, the tensions in social science as a whole were articulated over eighty years ago as: 'Two of the most characteristic features of modern psychology are (1) the special attention given to the facets of emotional consciousness and (2) the persistent endeavor to obtain a quantitative statement of results' (Brown, 1922: 7).

During the last decade or so, notions of different forms of intelligence (Gardner, 1983) including even an *emotional intelligence* (Goleman, 1995) have become popular. Previously, many procedures had been based upon an approach to a cognition that was essentially mechanical and linear; this has frequently been unhelpful in professional practice, for example, when working in complex situations with individual children and their families. The ways in which we had come to think about thinking had assumed the characteristics of the industrial society in which we lived. Also, many of our conceptualizations of thinking had come to view the mind's reasoning as not only linear and mechanical but pure, and crucially, this was distinct and separate from and also primary to our emotional life. We find this phenomenon predicted during the mid-nineteenth century: 'Thomas Carlyle warned ... that people would not only adapt mechanical processes of thought but come to believe that the mind itself was a machine' (Davis, 2002: 158).

Assuming the primacy of a mechanical kind of thinking has often affected a whole range of interventions with children. In schools there has sometimes been a rigid delivery of routine teaching programmes, for example, remedial approaches to reading which do not take account of the affective processes that underpin a child's enjoyment and motivation for what is essentially a social and cultural experience (Shaldon and Cullen, 2003).

There is, of course, a tradition of distinguished developmental psychologists who have been sensitive to the possibilities and potentials of more complex and inherently social models of child development, not only William James (1890), but Lev Vygotsky (1978, 1986), Margaret Donaldson (1978) and Jerome Bruner (1986). All too often, however, the default position for child psychologists in practice, for example, has been to assume the Cartesian notion of cognition first with emotion and the impact of our social worlds as both separate and secondary entities.

It could be argued that such theories and assumptions led to particular kinds of practices that often resulted in the segregation of children (Billington, 2000a). Indeed it could be argued that this was both the desire and the outcome of the very first testing regimes a century ago. Perhaps it is opportune now to look again at ways of thinking about children which accord with principles of human rights and increased client participation, but also in ways which in their very conceptual roots resist the processes of social fragmentation and exclusion and instead support social cohesion.

THEORIES IN PRACTICE

The division of labour between theory and practice is of course artificial. Any professional practice must be based on an idea or belief whilst an analysis of theoretical foundations will be vital to an understanding of any changes in practice.

The following, therefore, is a simple illustration of the ways in which professional theory-choice impacts upon children's lives;

it is perhaps a scenario which could be known to any one of us who work with children. In particular, this example highlights the limitations imposed by theoretical schisms between considerations of children's feelings, thinking and learning which are concretized in professional practices and institutions, organizations and systems.

Several years ago I was asked to provide a local education authority (LEA) with an assessment prior to the eventual issue of a Statement of Special Needs to a girl (aged 8) and a boy (aged 6). These were a sister and brother, 'Kelly' and 'Joe'. The progress of both children had been monitored closely by staff across health and education during their infant years, but it had become clear that they were now experiencing some literacy difficulties in school. It also became clear, however, that there were a number of other issues that might be relevant. For example, there was a thinly-veiled family history of turbulence and instability as well as grinding poverty, both economic and cultural.

At the time the outcome in such cases was predictable. One LEA concern is to achieve efficient management of its resources and as such it was effectively interested in defining the precise level of learning need. Usually in such cases this would mean that the children could be classified as having some sort of mild or moderate learning difficulty prior to their removal to a special needs class. This author, however, did not see any evidence either that the children wanted to move schools or indeed any evidence to suggest that such a move would lead to improved outcomes for them. The eventual decision allowed for some extra support from the area *dyslexia* team so the school was happy and the children were allowed to stay; a good deal all round, perhaps. I always suspected, however, that even by the end of the statutory process we had completely missed the point.

Subsequently, working as an independent psychologist, I was asked to provide a report on a family of children who were the subject of care proceedings brought by this same local authority (LA) against a mother and father. Reading through the files I discovered Kelly and Joe again, only this time together with their siblings. The different paperwork to which I now had access this time highlighted years of family instability, children out of control in the neighbourhood, as well as their mother's susceptibility to relationships with a string of ultimately violent men.

Now during the first assessment the culture within that part of the LA requesting my reports meant that they had not been interested in these children's experiences; indeed as far as education staff were concerned such experiences, if true, were regrettable but were not decisive factors in determining levels of educational support. Literacy difficulties after all were thought to fall straightforwardly within the cognitive domain.

Just two years later, however, that same LA, albeit a different branch of it, was now enthusiastic for any evidence that could be uncovered of emotional abuse and any other psychological scars that the children would have suffered as part of their experience of living with their mother and these men. Strangely, however, the LA did not seem interested in the need for continuity in the children's education or the importance of their progress in acquiring basic skills such as reading. Once again, the assessment processes were in danger of missing the point.

Social workers chose theories about Kelly and Joe which placed as primary their emotional needs and paid less attention to their thinking, learning and schooling. Education staff continued to focus on theories of learning and intelligence which took little heed of their emotional needs. As a consequence the children were in danger of being uprooted from both home and school.

Theory choice can thus lead professionals from different agencies to create different representations of a child, each based on a different kind of language. Breakdowns in communication between the various agencies are almost inevitable because they share neither a common language nor similar theory making about children (DoH, 2001a).

Clearly this was not the end of the story, either for these children or for this practitioner, but it is necessary to contain the limits of the narrative here within the overall thrust of the chapter and offer a conclusion as to the ways in which professional disputes can erupt. Simplistically, the social services' department was interested primarily in the emotional lives of the children while education staff were interested primarily in the children's *cognition* or *learning difficulties*. Many will have seen such contests degenerate into funding disputes between employees within the same organization. It should be noted once again, however, that this author's own position afforded a privileged vantage point from which to conduct such an analysis. This position is likely to reflect more the power of individual professionals (for example as 'expert') rather than support any claim to singular truths.

Nevertheless, in the care proceedings it became possible to sustain arguments in which the children's emotional needs and their potential for learning were so inter-connected that they were considered inseparable. Perhaps this is a gestalt that should not too easily be split asunder, not only in other cases but in training curricula (see also Billington, in Billington and Pomerantz, 2004).

FEELING, THINKING AND LEARNING

In the radio discussion between Bate, the English scholar, Hobson, the psychiatrist and Greenfield, the neuroscientist, their common ground was not merely that they were viewing cognition and our affective lives as somehow connected but that they too were viewing them as absolutely inseparable. Such views are supported by others:

> the bizarre distinction between cognition and emotion, as if somehow one could have thoughts without emotion, a mind without affect ... [Feelings] are just as cognitive as any other percept, but what makes them different is that they are first and foremost about the body, that they offer us the cognition of our internal milieu, visceral, and musculoskeletal states ... Feelings are the first step in letting us mind the body. (Damasio, 2001, in Bate, 2003: 14)

While such contemporary research is suggesting that the processes of feeling and thinking are inseparable, nearly two hundred years ago the poet William Wordsworth may have anticipated this same relationship 'intuitively', again challenging simplistic divisions of labour in claims to knowledge:

> For Wordsworth ... it is emotion that awakens and alerts the faculty of mind. (Bate, 2003: 13)

The twist is that both the nineteenth-century poet and the contemporary neuroscientist suggest that thinking does not have primacy over feeling. Just what would be the implications should our thinking about children be based, not on the simplistic supremacy of the cognitive inherited from the all-pervasive Cartesian tradition of "I think, therefore, I am", but to build our work instead on a different premise which can be framed initially as "I feel and think, therefore I am"?

The time is now right to consider the consequences of placing the child's emotional well-being as of paramount importance whatever the presenting adult concern, whether in relation to their learning, their behaviour or indeed a particular psychopathology. So no matter what the presenting concerns, the responsibility of the professional would be to consider the impact of any direct work upon the child's emotional life because this will impact on their ability to think and thus to learn.

The model is not yet complete since it fails to take into account:

> The tools of thought are constructed on the basis of an infant's emotional engagement with other people. To put it bluntly, if an infant were not involved with other people, then she would not come to think. (Hobson, 2002: xiv)

and

> The very means to thinking may be interpersonal relations ... . (Hobson, 2002: 104)

Another contemporary researcher/practitioner suggests a way which leads again perhaps to a 'synergy' by articulating the inherently social ways in which children develop and function, articulated by Michael Rutter in the following way;

> Much of the variation between people stems from the synergistic combination of nature and nurture ... What really matters is not the relative strength of genetic and environmental effects but the mechanisms by which they exert their effects. Therein lies the future ... '(Rutter, 2002: 32)

A final dictum that might provide practitioners with the basis for a different theory choice when working with children might be:

> I feel and think *in-relation-to* another (that is, as a social being or *object*): therefore I am.

What kind of professional curriculum would be constructed if this were a first premise of evidence-based policies and interventions? How would this affect the ways in which we all *speak with, speak of* and *write about children?*

NOTES FOR THE FUTURE

In working with children we need to ensure that a new generation of theories about children and childhood builds upon lessons learned about children's feeling and thinking:

> Sullivan portrayed the early interactions between the infant and it's human environment as shaping an almost infinitely malleable collection of human potentials to fit an interpersonal ride to which that potential becomes finely adapted. (Fonagy, 2001: 126)

At the same time we could consider the evidence from traditional empirical research. Interestingly, neuroscientific research, for example, has the potential to support what artists, philosophers and 'lay-people' have always known or intuited: that the quality of our learning and thinking is inextricably linked to our world of feelings and emotional well-being.

> Emotion and related reactions are aligned with the body, feelings with the mind ... bodily emotions become the kind of thoughts we call feelings ... provide a privileged view into mind and body, [which are] the overtly disparate manifestations of a single and seemingly interwoven human organism. (Damasio, 2004: 7)

This perspective demands that in all aspects of our work with children, whether in a direct relationship or in consultation with parents or teachers, we would always have as a first concern the young person's feelings and emotional well-being. Again, there is nothing necessarily new here, for we have all long been aware of the importance of affect in children's lives, but to make more explicit the links between a child's ability to learn and their emotional lives would seem to be important work. It would resist, for example, the very idea of a simple intelligence, hitherto largely narrowly conceived, and demand rather that professionals do not retreat too hastily from the boundaries between simplicity and complexity, for example, in assessments of children.

> Bion's model for thinking suggests that real thinking, intelligence and learning occur whenever we are able to tolerate the sensations which accompany the incoming stimuli. He suggests that for learning to take place we must be able to tolerate the frustration (feeling) that results from working with living material. (Billington, 2000a: 112)

Now Bion is here providing a theory-based way back to the place from whence the social sciences came and it could be argued that mainstream psychology has achieved very little in the field of emotional consciousness and indeed that psychoanalysis has pursued this quest more honestly. However, should modern technology allow approaches to be adopted now in a way that merely encourages once again the simplistic application of rank, measurement and category, then a great opportunity will have been lost. To have repaired the theoretical schism only to more effectively subject children to new regimes of testing (of their emotional lives) would of course maintain power relationships between children and adults and support oppressive forms of governmentality, for example by invoking yet again the processes of marginalization and exclusion.

Trainee teachers or psychologists, for example, would not be taught to consider the individual facets or characteristics of a child as being separate from questions related to their overall (social) well-being which should always be paramount. Trainee social workers on the other hand could be allowed to gain the confidence to place the young person's ability to learn as central. As professionals, therefore, we could remain aware of the complexities in children's feelings and thinking processes and find better ways of representing learning processes as being essentially within the affective domain.

While consciousness itself may well be the Holy Grail for neuroscientific research in the twenty first century, the complex relationships between children's feelings, thinking and learning known to us already through professional practice provide another important site for development. However, I would propose that we will be able to work with renewed confidence only if we can seek to eliminate those practices which pathologize children whilst taking no account of the consequences for their emotional lives of any subsequent stigmatization or social exclusion.

Damasio's research suggests that there is growing evidence to confirm William James's assertion that 'feelings are necessarily a perception of the actual body changed by emotion'; given access to new technologies Damasio suggests also that feelings 'arise ... from the actual maps constructed at any given moment in the body-sensing regions ... ' (Damasio, 2004: 112). The outcomes of his research suggest that feelings are poised at the very threshold that separates being from knowing and thus have a privileged connection to consciousness. (Damasio, 2000: 50)

Our work with children and young people is clearly privileged but we need to adjust to the demands of children's services by encouraging in our work both professional practices and 'educational systems [which emphasize] unequivocal connections between current feelings and future outcomes' (Damasio, 2000: 247).

The first principles for a new era of working with children could be based on a growing sensitivity to the rights, potentials and narratives of individual children and young people as well as evidence from contemporary neuroscience, but always highlighting rather than obscuring a need to work with the inevitable tensions that arise in critiques of power and authority in children's lives. Together, these could provide some of the foundations for a totally reconstructed training and development curriculum for those working with children and young people.

Our success at the individual level, however, will also depend on the quality of our relationships with children and young people, for whether as social worker, teacher, health professional or psychologist we engage in these relationships, which are at the core of all social science practice. As such we could ensure that we do not merely subscribe to the principles of ethical codes but work hard to resist becoming separated from matters of social justice which, of course, are the preserve of all human history.

Traditionally, education has been the preserve of the cognitive in children's lives while social services have tended to colonize the discourses of children's emotional lives. Perhaps empirical science is at last in a position to address those questions which prompted the very foundation of the social sciences to provide care and education and in the process could at last heal epistemological wounds.

However, the ways in which social sciences absorb any oppressive agendas will not only require criticality on the part of its practitioners, but political awareness and judgement.

FURTHER READING

Bion, W. R. (1962) *Learning from Experience*. London: Heinemann.
Bion, W. R. (1970) *Attention and Interpretation*. London: Tavistock.

Damasio, A. (1994) *Descartes' Error: Emotion, reason and the human brain*. New York: Quill.

Damasio, A. (2000) *The Feeling of What Happens: Body emotion and the making of consciousness*. London: Vintage.

Hobson, P. (2002) *The Cradle of Thought: Exploring the origins of thinking*. London: Macmillan.

James, W. (1980) *The Principles of Psychology*. New York: Holt, Rinehart and Winston.

Reflexive Activity

Select a young person with whom you work and speak about them to a colleague. Ask the colleague to identify the points at which you prioritized specific theoretical explanations of their functioning or of the situation. What other theoretical explanations were excluded in your account? Note the consequences of omitting possibilities.

7 VOICES OF CHILDREN AND YOUNG PEOPLE IN ASSESSMENT

The two principle frameworks providing the legislative contexts for the assessment of children and young people in England and Wales during the last twenty years have been Education Acts (1981, 1995 and 2004) and, since the protection of children has become more recognized as being of concern to the whole of our society, the Children Acts (1989 and 2004). Care and education, therefore, have provided the two arenas in which children and their needs could be discussed and assessed.

Given public disquiet in respect of all the issues raised in certain high profile cases, all sorts of dilemmas have been played out in media accounts which have served as a focus for wider social debate about what we regard as the nature of childhood itself (for example, questions about the age at which children became criminally or sexually responsible). While we have no evidence that children are actually any more vulnerable to unscrupulous adults than in times past and while it is arguable whether as a population children are more vulnerable than other groups to governmental scrutiny in the present (for example the elderly), as a category of human being (the boundaries of which are always subject to negotiation) children are not allowed the same recourse to democratic processes.

The imbalance in rights and responsibilities by comparison with the rest of the population was recognized globally to some extent by the *United Nations Convention on the Rights of the Child* (UNICEF, 1989), which was eventually ratified by the British government in 1991. Article 12 of the convention, in particular, has been influential in extending democratic potentials to young people in its requirement that they should be consulted on any matter related to their needs, a principle endorsed in England and Wales by the Special Needs and Disability Act (HMSO, 2001).

Organizing professional practices by using this simple principle has not proved easy, however, since these evolved originally when many people (not just children), allotted to a particular category, could be denied rights at crucial moments in their lives. Gender, ethnicity and social class have been arbiters of acceptable modes of living, while those classified as 'disabled' (physically or intellectually) and many other social groups besides have all at various times been subject to marginalization and disenfranchisement. Unfortunately some past professional practices often served not to liberate such people from the oppression of their circumstances, but were utilized to justify decisions whereby government could be dispensed with and which effectively restricted democratic freedoms.

Currently, however, professionals are being confronted with accounts of experience in various media which have been produced by people who had previously been thus disempowered. As a result, for example, qualities of ability and intelligence in those individuals are becoming evident where previously they had not been recognized. Also, as suggested during the previous chapter, professional theory choices are adjusting to new conditions in which the boundaries between expert knowledge and client experience are being challenged and negotiated.

The 1989 Children Act was in many respects a unique piece of social legislation. It was undoubtedly a human response to the outcries during the 1980s about how some children were being forced to live their lives, that is to say in situations defined as abusive. The act attempted to create legal contexts which supported the protection of children in a less adversarial fashion and would be family friendly in their manner of execution. While clearly not perfect the main thrust behind the 1989 Act, which was to protect children and young people from harm, has not yet been subject to sustained opposition.

The Common Assessment Framework (DfES, 2005) is another development which has been designed to build on the principles of protection and rights enshrined in the Children Act and the UN Convention. There have been some further significant changes in recent legislation, for example in the Children Act (2004), relating to children's understanding of and responsibility in criminal matters. Nevertheless the underlying position taken by legislation remains in that some children suffer harm while in the care of adults and thus are in need of the protection of the state.

Clearly, the issues covered by the Children Act are complex and a critique is beyond the scope of this chapter or indeed this book. However, the UN Convention and the 1989 Children Act were absolutely vital in demanding of professionals and services that efforts should be made to extend democratic rights as far as possible to young people, manifest especially in the assertion that children should be consulted in matters affecting them. The 'voice of the child' as it is now commonly known is a theme running through these remaining chapters.

PUBLIC AND PRIVATE LAW

Professionals can be asked to assess children's welfare under the specific direction of the courts and while this occurs more usually within public law it can occur also in private law. Public law, for example, relates to the care, protection or placement of young people and is usually invoked by a local authority which typically sets before the court arguments that a child should be removed from the care of their parents on account of a range of factors within a framework of abuse defined as emotional, physical, sexual or neglect. Private law typically provides a framework to settle disputes between family members, invariably following family breakdown, and relates to access and contact issues.

Local authority social workers in practice tend only to be involved in public law matters. However, independent social workers and psychologists can be asked to provide assessments across the legal framework. Specific issues covered are wide ranging, from children's daily living arrangements (and all that these entail) and contact with various family members, to health matters and education. Officers from CAFCASS (the Children and Family Court Advisory Service) are the main professional resource for the courts in child and family proceedings (incorporating Children's Guardians as well as Child and Family Court Welfare Officers).

CAFCASS professionals have been allocated the core role in assisting the court to arrive at decisions which accord with the important legislative requirement in proceedings that the 'child's welfare is paramount'. Professionals from this organization always seem to have embraced that principle enthusiastically and have looked to utilize fully subsequent frameworks of assessment such as the Welfare Checklist (Children Act 1989: s.1 (3). Also in my experience this particular group of professionals can be relatively free from those day-to-day economic pressures often faced by those of us who work for other agencies when arriving at important opinions. CAFCASS workers are well-positioned to provide advocacy for a young person in ensuring that their needs and wishes can be respected, even when this brings them into conflict with parents for example.

Together with the involvement of a CAFCASS officer, a child in public law proceedings is appointed their own solicitor who is employed to act in their best interests which may at times conflict with the views of a local authority, for example, or indeed the parents. The child's solicitor and the guardian should work closely together, explaining both their roles and the court processes to the young person and consulting with them to ascertain their views. This work has invariably been conducted in what has seemed to me to be a most respectful manner and this has served as a contrast to practices in other arenas where the power relationships between adult and child do not always so easily promote respect for the wishes of the child (for example, in school or at home). Sometimes, however, a young person can express an opinion about their own situation with which the guardian cannot agree and on these occasions the child's solicitor and the guardian are required to act separately in articulating the child's needs and wishes. This distinction seems to mark a significant advance in the extension of democratic principles.

However, there are several drawbacks in all of this, not least that a child can still endure months or even years of professional investigation (and perhaps abuse) before they are afforded such respect, time and advocacy. Also, in the vast majority of proceedings, children are not allowed to present their own evidence in court and they are therefore vulnerable to the ability of adult professionals to represent both them and their wishes. Again, it is not the intention here to critique in detail the processes of

Children Act legislation since the issues of children's rights and responsibilities which justify professional responses in such matters are clearly complex.

At this point, however, I am more concerned with addressing not the extent of children's participation in care proceedings but specifically the ability of professionals, in my case as a psychologist, to address the tricky issue of how to represent the child – not in the sense of being an advocate, but in the sense of the extent to which any professional can create in an assessment a 'true' portrait of the young person. This, of course, returns us to the core issues in the book encapsulated by the five question-themes posed earlier: how do we speak of children? how do we speak with children? how do we write of children? how do we listen to children? how do we listen to ourselves (when working with children)?

LEGISLATIVE CONTEXTS OF ASSESSMENT

During past employment by a local authority I was often required to provide assessments of children and young people under Education Act legislation. The need to assess was often justified in terms of a young person's special needs, whether social, emotional, behavioural or learning, a disability of some kind, or perhaps connected to a particular syndrome, for example autism.

Now while professional activities were governed ultimately by primary legislation (here the 1989 Children Act) and a demand that advice was provided in accordance with the welfare of the child, it was sometimes difficult when providing this advice not to remain mindful of the interests of the employers (in my case the local authority), or indeed other powerful adult voices in the community – for example headteachers, parents or particular vested interest or lobby groups. Indeed it was a vital part of the assessment that such voices were heard within the assessment process.

However, by contrast, the voice of the child could be faint if heard at all and frequently the thrust of professional assessment activities would not be directed primarily towards eliciting such views. Clearly, there were (and still are) at the very least technical difficulties in accessing the views of some young people, whether on account of their age or particular form of special need or disability however defined (Griffiths, 2002). In retrospect, whilst sometimes these difficulties seemed insurmountable, the very nature of the professional activities themselves seemed designed to restrict or exclude the possibility of participation by the young person. Professional practices seemed to be constructed on the assumption that the young person would either not have a voice, or even if they did that it would be of lesser importance in arriving at a final opinion.

Quite apart from the earlier story of Michael in Chapter 4, in which human understanding had looked to survive professional training, at about the same time I was fortunate to attend a conference at which Ruth Marchant presented her work (Marchant and Waller, 1992). The graphic portrayal of situations in which young people with disabilities could become subject to (usually unwitting) humiliations as a regular part of daily life when in contact with adult professionals and carers was unforgettable. The sense of shame evoked in me in respect of my own professional practices was so strong that it served to inform my professional decision making thereafter. The invisibility sometimes of the young people to adults in the performance of professional duties could not be denied and, of course, this allows comparison with the experience of other marginalized groups who might similarly be invisible one minute and then the subject of professional scrutiny the next (see for example Spender, 1989; Gallego, 2006).

In conducting those assessments for an education authority, it often seemed that the analyses were incomplete and that important areas were being overlooked when considering the whole range of a child's needs. In the case of Kelly and Joe in Chapter 6 the focus of the first assessment had been on the children's learning difficulties, while the same local authority in the form of its social services subsequently wanted to focus on any kind of harm suffered by the children while in the care of the parent.

It seemed that in the course of both assessments that an important point was being missed. In concentrating on their learning alone vital clues were being missed in relation to the general well-being of the children. When concentrating solely on alleged emotional harm suffered by the children, the restorative effects of good educational provision and the need to develop potentials were in danger of being overlooked. In Chapter 2, I also referred to the case of Callum in which I had insisted that a removal from the care of his parents should not be compounded by a simultaneous removal from his chosen school (see Billington in Billington and Pomerantz, 2004, for more detailed analysis).

It is precisely in response to such manufactured contests, for example between the demands of different agencies, that the British government has acted quite rightly to look at all the ways in which children are assessed and to see whether any common principles can be identified. After several years, the Common Assessment Framework (DFES, 2005) has been devised and conceived as a means of reducing possible inter-professional confusions and this is to be adopted by agencies by 2008.

There are many exemplary principles contained within this document, not least in its acceptance of the need to consult with young people but especially in its exhortation for professionals to find a 'common language'. This seems absolutely right and proper especially when agencies have clearly struggled to communicate with each other effectively in the past, with tragic consequences (Laming, 2003). Furthermore, while professionals have as described earlier operated according to a division of labour in respect of both practical and theoretical issues when considering children, technological developments have recently been made which suggest that some theoretical rapprochement might be achieved which may support the implementation of the CAF (that is, between feeling and thinking, care and education; see Chapter 6).

Yet in seeking to conduct effective yet ethical assessments a danger arises here that some monolithic practice might emerge which serves to restrict any opposition or resistance to a 'received wisdom', which would presumably be controlled by government. The division of labour, while often generating such inter-professional conflict and confusion, has in fact been useful in stimulating the emergence of new knowledges and the threat to the evolution of new knowledge therefore is clear. While the sheer scope of the assessment task might begin to seem overwhelming regarding the complexity of issues to take into consideration, it is surely a mistake merely to silence difference and disagreement, for this needs to be encouraged if we are to develop a range of practices capable of robustly addressing the range of (changing) needs.

CONTEXTS FOR ASSESSMENTS IN CHILDREN ACT PROCEEDINGS

In receiving instructions from the courts a quite wonderful paradox becomes apparent for, while being accorded the respect and privilege of being able to provide an opinion on a matter of vital importance in the life of a young person, a crucial principle arises from which there is no escape. For in accepting such instructions good practice requires (and the court demands) that not only should the basis of such opinion be made clear, but the limits of one's knowledge too should be defined. Further, it is made absolutely transparent to all that whatever one says or writes it is never the role of the 'expert' to pronounce a truth but merely an opinion, and that any 'truth' remains solely the preserve of the court and specifically in the hands of the judge (Wall, 2000).

From the outside the legal system might appear daunting, imbued as it is with a sense of exclusivity and privilege. However, such checks and balances exist within the system that an 'expert' opinion (as distinct from any claim to 'truth') independent of all parties can only be provided in the Children Act by adhering strictly to the principle that the child's well-being remains paramount above all other considerations. A professional's responsibility is directly to the court which will be the ultimate arbiter of a child's best interests. These are clearly heavy restrictions but in the binds of practice there remains professional freedom and some clarity.

The issues to be dealt with, on the other hand, are invariably anything but simple. Complexity and messiness are the norm in situations which are invariably beyond the wit of any single professional or agency to resolve. Assessment, therefore, has not only to be sufficiently robust but also sensitive and sophisticated in order to meet these demands. The CAF does indeed provide an excellent basis for assessment and a clear sense of direction to the professional as to the issues to be considered when compiling assessments which help not just government but young people. The triangular template it employs is an effective visual resource and the specifications are comprehensive at the level of the individual.

Issues are once again framed by matters connected to care, health and education and the five outcomes mentioned previously (DfES, 2005) once again provide a useful target for professional achievement. The way in which my own assessment practice has evolved has similarly recognized the necessity of juxtaposing information acquired from a wide variety of sources; for example, from family members, from teachers, social workers, play workers, other psychologists or medical practitioners. Sometimes there are mountains of documentation to absorb while on other occasions there is little previous recorded professional knowledge.

Always, however, my intention is to create a history and a context for the life which is being lived by the child. Clearly, the young person themselves should have much to contribute to this and I contend that the spirit of our times suggests that professional practices must be organized according to ethical approaches in this respect and in keeping with democratic principles. Sometimes I continue to use psychological tests, for example ability tests or those which look at family relations, as a means of generating sources of information in line with my own professional interests. Always though, it is the young person's approach to such tests – the manner of their performance, as opposed to any specific results for example – which are most significant, for once again it is the relationships emerging between the young person and the materials (as transitional objects) and also the young person and myself (in the transitional space) which are the core concern of ethical practices.

In my view any adult working with a young person has to adopt, before all else, an imaginative stance in which they primarily seek to consider not merely the needs of the child before them but their own wishes too. It is a matter of clear professional responsibility therefore, to consider the question-theme, 'how do we listen to ourselves?' Before that process can begin, or rather as part of the early stages itself, we need to consider likely questions that a young person might need answering. For example, who on earth does a young person think the professional is? Can they really have any understanding of the differences between a social worker, a guardian or a psychologist when many adults struggle to define the different roles?

Also, what can a young person know of the purpose of a session/assessment? Clearly as professionals we are not family and so what rationale does a young person employ in order to understand the social context of the meeting? Just what is expected of them? What are the rules which they would look to either observe or transgress? What will success look like or failure?

An older child with good language abilities will make it easier obviously for the professional to work with these tricky issues, but younger children or those who are less able to engage in conversation for whatever reason present us with problems. For how can we know the wishes or thoughts of a young person who is unable to communicate them? Indeed a more fundamental issue begins to emerge; to what extent should professionals, in fulfilment of ethical or democratic principles, intrude in a life in order to find out the answers to their questions?

While such dilemmas can become overwhelming for the professional sometimes there are young people for whom the issues are quite simple, for example, they merely wish to be returned to their parent, perhaps remain in school or else need to be safe. Some other children will have become accustomed to dealing with professionals and after a lifetime of being observed and assessed they may be only too aware of the issues and are thus able to predict exactly what they should say to get a desired result. To make things more complicated the simple ploy of saying what they feel needs to be said can sometimes serve to mask the seriousness of the issues confronting a young person, which may appear irresolvable and/or unbearable (for example by resisting or refusing adult attempts to communicate).

In working according to the principles of the Children Act, the intervention of a professional in the life of a young person is unusual and not something which as yet can be taken for granted. Teachers are perhaps in a special relationship with young people but what is the primary justification for the involvement of other professionals, for example social workers or health workers? In the case of matters before a court, practices are determined usually to protect a child in some way, when the latter is deemed by the court to be at risk of harm whether physical or psychological.

While the needs of a young person are considered paramount, however, accessing these views proves to be not so straightforward.

As stated earlier in the chapter, only rarely is a young person invited into the court and asked for their views, a position which is determined largely by two founding principles. First of all, there is a view in law that a young person below a certain age is not capable of understanding or being responsible in a number of respects. Secondly, it is deemed that there are professionals employed by governmental agencies of one kind or another who are expert in working with children in ways which allow them to elicit their views and which in the process do not compound any harm already affecting the child.

Indeed, while a young person may not be able to articulate their wishes skilful professional practice can sometimes create conditions in which they may feel more able to express their true wishes and feelings, whether through language, through other (non-verbal) responses to issues raised during the assessment relationship or even during testing.

The core principle here is that children will already have constructed a particular perception of their situation and the vast majority will have an understanding of their position, however unlikely or different from ours that may seem. What becomes problematic is when a young person chooses to hold on to a view which would leave them exposed to some kind of danger. In practice this can be quite common; for example, a young person who has not only become used to caring for a drug-abusing parent, but who has organized and constructed their whole way of being and looking at the world in order to protect a loved one or to justify an existing way of living. In order to change their views in such cases a child might have to totally reassess their sense of identity and belonging, especially where removal from home would elicit feelings of disloyalty and protection.

In other cases where a child's views could place them in some danger, preventing the young person from providing testimony in the court can actually serve as protection itself, for example where the expression of wishes might lead to a child being psychologically squeezed via the demands of warring parents or else being overwhelmed by the pressure of considering conflicting ideas about a situation. Indeed some children might feel compelled to hold on to a particular point of view, especially when having to deal with any memories of harm perpetrated upon them by a family member or trusted adult. In these situations, therefore, the ways in which children's views are accessed and subsequently represented to the court become the sole responsibility of the professional.

PRINCIPLES OF ASSESSMENT

The CAF is more than a template – it is a social construction whereby the terms and conditions for thinking about and assessing children are defined. As such it does not merely affect practice but instead codifies a theoretical knowledge about child development, learning and well-being. Indeed it serves to articulate government views about childhood within our society. What theoretical resources can be amassed, therefore, in supporting assessment practices which attend to the principles of extending democratization, involving participants and resisting social exclusion, while at the same time ensuring the protection of children and encouraging their development to maximum potential?

Rather than learning only about 'disorders', 'difficulties', or other conditions, I would suggest that professionals working with children should more than ever before be able to identify with precision the evidence upon which their opinion is based at any particular point. This evidence base might be provided by research literature, whether quantitative or qualitative, empirical or theoretical, and subsequently appraised in the light of professional experience.

Beyond this it is not merely the individual research 'finding' or professional knowledge which is important, but the internal cohesion of the professional argument which is reached by recourse both to research and professional judgment in applying specialist knowledge to particular circumstances. The specific context of any assessment will be determined by the unique positions of various participants in relation to one another within a particular case – the assessor, the person to be assessed and a whole host of other variables which always in social science research prevent us from ever going beyond probability.

Social science research is of necessity fundamentally different from material science research, since while results from data can sometimes be generalized to a limited extent they rarely achieve the power of prediction in individual cases. This is because the sheer volume of variables to be accounted for, both in research and practice, make working with children potentially so problematic. One of these variables, of course, will be the particular ways in which the power differentials are manifest between parties. While there is little immediate hope or realistic ambition that a true 'equality' might be achieved between the assessor and assessed, professional and child, there is simply no justification now for a professional to act without an analysis of the power relationships as well as the contextual factors in a case.

Often in Children Act proceedings the documentation can be extensive, but frequently still not comprehensive enough. Assessment in practice, therefore, relies on the commitment of a professional to accessing all possible forms of data in a manner which achieves the principle of 'least possible intrusion'. Invariably I like to meet not only with the child but with other family members and the other professionals involved. In particular I usually prefer to see the child in a school situation, especially in the case of care proceedings as this would hopefully be a source of some stability, for example, in terms of social relationships. Judy Dunn's work (Dunn, 2004) is especially helpful in reminding us of the importance of peer and sibling relationships, since these offer special sources of support which encourage the development of resilience through the continuity of normalizing social relations.

It can take several meetings and weeks of contemplation before even one essential element can offer itself as a crystallizing and central feature in a case. While it might help some people to create a visual map of the issues, whether individual or historical for example, I prefer to hold the situation and all its variables almost at a felt, emotional level. In Luke's case (Chapter 5) this allowed me to feel something of his mother's lack of self-confidence as well as her determination to stick by her son despite his apparent rejection. It allowed me also, to sense something of Peter's plight, although I hypothesized that this was a far more difficult place to go and therefore limited the scope of any identification.

Crucially, however, it allowed me to feel the full weight of Luke's evidence when, in that safe space I had created with him, he could reflect on the changes in relation between the two protagonists which he described as, 'it changed from my mum battling for me to my mum battling [Peter] ... I just want everyone to get on ...'

The way in which assessment constitutes an intervention is seen clearly here, for once having been allowed to form a view it cannot be totally eradicated. As such there will forever be a part of Luke who is able to construct a view of a situation where it was the adults, not him who held responsibility. In day-to-day living he had been trying to achieve a middle course between these two adults and would invariably fail in his aim. Taking such responsibility is a monumental task for a young person but one attempted by many who are desperate to remain loyal to their attachment figures. The space created with Luke during assessment, however, had allowed him to identify a particular resource in himself that would enable him if he chose to absolve himself of some of that responsibility.

Engaged in a similar analysis of her own practice as a clinical psychologist, Sam Warner has found that, 'I build up a comprehensive context for making judgments by triangulating different types and sources of information (written, spoken and enacted with myself and regarding observation of others)'. She refers to her own assessment reports as 'critical construction reports' and her experience accords with my own in stating that while 'necessarily long-winded because they do not rely on reductive psychometric formulations ... those in civil procedures welcome such reports because they contextualize information ...' (Warner, forthcoming).

Clearly in any assessment there are many complex issues to be considered when determining the precise activities of the professional in working with a young person. In the last two chapters I shall continue in search of those practices which might restrict rather than compound the level of harm being suffered by an individual child.

In brief, in assessing young people we need to:

- acknowledge the complexities in everyday human behaviour and learning;
- resist the automatic use of simplistic, linear, problem-solving models;
- be aware of the impact of our own presence within our work;
- work with the important adults in children's lives in order to assist them to achieve the changes which too often are only demanded of the children themselves;

- separate the needs of individuals, child and adult, within practices;
- identify power relations as a crucial factor which can determine psychological practices;
- resist the pressures which require us often to conceive of a child within the constraints of narrow and social contexts or else influenced by administrative or economic imperatives;
- work with lived experience, our own and that of the young person with whom we are working (Billington, 1995: 44).

Reflexive Activity

Consider a young person with whom you have been working. What issues could you have focused on differently given alternative institutional priorities and methods of service delivery? How could your practice and theory choice have been different if you were working within another professional system?

8 WORKING WITH AUTISTIC CHILDREN

Autism studies invite some fundamental considerations about the ways in which we all come to feel, think and learn in the world; how we make sense of our experience; think more deeply about what human perception, or human relations, or human intelligence, or human language, or human creativity, actually are. (Hobson, 2002: 182)

In this chapter, the ways in which a particular psychopathology can be constructed according to certain preferred knowledges are explored. Services and professional practices have evolved which have traditionally excluded clients from owning a knowledge of themselves. The location of knowledge is changing, however, and there are challenges ahead for support agencies and professionals when planning policies and practices.

During the last twenty years a more complex understanding of autism has emerged (Frith, 1989, 2003; Baron-Cohen et al., 1993; Jordan et al., 1998; Happe, 1999; Hobson, 2002). More recently, however, some autistic people have themselves begun to write at length about their lives and experiences. Where previously many of us had not searched for more imaginative ways of understanding, writers such as Clare Sainsbury (2000) and Kenneth Hall (2001), as well as a host of others, have begun to educate us in the hitherto largely unknown and perhaps until recently largely unsuspected life and energy within many autistic minds.

Yet the very nature of the social communication of autistic young people renders difficult full implementation of emancipatory or democratizing principles and practices. And at the same time the extent to which any characteristic functioning might be exacerbated by the operational modes of current services has not been the focus of extensive research.

Autism has, however, undoubtedly captured the imagination of public and professionals alike. Why is this? Like Peter Hobson, I would suggest that it is because we are fascinated by the questions posed by autism and their capacity to strike at the very heart of us, for they are questions which challenge us to contemplate our own mind and our own consciousness. When we meet an autistic child, therefore, we may not merely be confronted by their deficits or impairments but our own. Here are some observations therefore, based on my own clinical work:

- rigid adherence to simplistic interpretations of the autistic 'triad of impairments' in communication, interaction and imagination (Wing, 1996) can in practice lead inadvertently to the development of services and professional practices that struggle to address the needs of those children who are identified (as well as their families);
- the models of social deficit often employed to depict autistic children are themselves impaired in their ability to conceptualize individual experience, 'I believe in differences in autism rather than disability in autism' (Sinclair, 2004);
- 'insider' accounts may provide professionals with a valuable source of information when creating services and developing practices (Avdi et al., 2000; Billington et al., 2000).

Many conventional approaches in education and social care mean that it is difficult to accommodate easily the differences presented by those young people regarded as autistic. The difficulties faced by the professional are considerable and under such conditions the practices of problem identification and diagnosis flourish. During previous unpublished community-based research with parents, however (Billington, 2000b), it became clear that while many sought a diagnosis for their child, in the main this was only because it was the most effective way of accessing professional services. What parents had really wanted was help, support and understanding – and much earlier (Billington et al., 2000). The diagnosis therefore is a complex social intervention which, while imparted by the professional in a few seconds, can affect both the lives of the parents and also the child's life for the rest of their days.

What relief to the hard-pressed teacher, parent or young person, therefore, who after months or years of disappointment, feelings of failure or social disapproval suddenly discovers explanations that provide reassurances and soothe raw feelings. For descriptions of autism invariably attempt to tidy up the condition and are usually offered in forms which allow the harassed individual a place to rest in an otherwise de-stabilized and at times seemingly irrational autistic world. (Billington, 2005: 6)

But just what are autistic spectrum disorders?

PROFESSIONAL VOICES

The 'official' definitions were agreed by psychiatrists either within the Diagnostic and Statistical Manual of the American Psychiatrists Association (American Psychiatric Association, 1994) and the International Classification and Diagnosis manual (ICD-10), while the British Psychological Society is currently publishing its own position paper (BPS, forthcoming). However, professional accounts tend to differ markedly from the accounts of autistic people (see Billington, 2000a); in light of this consider the following two extracts which purport to depict aspects of autism:

Marked impairments in the use of multiple, non-verbal behaviours such as eye-to-eye gaze, facial expression, body postures and gestures to regulate social interaction ... failure to develop peer relationships appropriate to developmental level ... a lack of spontaneous seeking to share enjoyment, interests or achievements ... lack of social or emotional reciprocity. (American Psychiatric Association, 1994)

... bewilderment; isolated; absorption; lonely; puzzlement; sensitive; confused; emotional; routine; interesting; frightened; fear; rigid; intelligent; anxious; confused; unsure; compulsive; ritualistic; bleak; sad; intelligence; strength; distant; safety (need for); escape (need for); angry; frustrating; flapping; idiosyncratic; incoherent; obsessive; unaware of others; unhappy; wilful; alone; aggressive; unrestrained; honest; passive; anxiety; imitative; literal; abrupt; affectionate; something about humour; perceptive. (Billington, 2001: 4)

While the above may present a false dichotomy, which form of representation would we choose as a basis for providing advice or training? In my experience, the former undoubtedly tends to be the official or 'dominant' story, but opportunities to articulate and express other descriptions in professional practice have often been of interest to teachers and parents and have, on occasion, provided the basis for more person-centred interventions with the young people themselves. Indeed, the list of words above was not created by me but by teachers who had autistic children in their classes and who had been asked to provide words which they thought best described the autistic children with whom they were working. Clearly, some of the words were not simply descriptions of the children but could have been projections of the teachers' own feelings. However, the absence of any *lack of* is marked by comparison with 'official' definitions. The deficit model is not so apparent while the words often provide evidence of the capacity of professionals, in this case teachers, to consider positively the qualitative aspects of a human being.

In case work rather than any specific impairments, stereotypy or deficits, it has invariably been the strength of the feelings present that has been one of the most striking features, in particular the distress expressed by many of the family members and other professionals engaged directly. It has sometimes been difficult to avoid a further hypothesis that the autistic child may at times also experience overwhelming, unbearable and painful feelings.

Many professionals have often seemed to be more at ease in addressing children's 'behaviour' rather than their emotional lives but the evidence of the teachers above suggests a potential for a more human response. However, I would argue here that it would have been easier for them (sometimes by sheer necessity) to draw upon theoretical resources that would engage only secondarily with the nature of these children's experiences. Indeed the language in relation to ASDs perpetrated by many specialists can serve only too easily to de-humanize both the people and the issues which are the subjects of enquiry.

I would suggest that any understanding of a child's difficulties which as professionals we might have and therefore the appropriateness of our advice may well be dependent on our ability to have some insight or understanding of the child's experiences, in particular those of intense feeling, rather than any search for failure. "Insider" accounts have themselves begun to present new challenges to accepted '"expert" positions, many sharing the claim that "the real experts are those people with autism"' (Exley, in Hesmondhalgh and Breakey, 2001: 10).

Donna Williams (1992) used words about herself – for example *afraid, gentle, magical* – which are not only her property, for they are words which any of us might choose to use about ourselves or one another. As such, they would not be sufficient to support ideas of autistic 'abnormality', 'emotional unresponsiveness' or 'rigidity'. Indeed her words, referring as they do to her emotional and expressive life, seem to have little in common with traditional explanations of autism.

It is not only the way in which a popular perception of emotional unresponsiveness can be dispelled that is remarkable, however, but rather the degree of emotional sensitivity which autistic writers often claim for themselves, writing at length of their emotional hypersensitivity (see for example Jolliffe et al., 1992; Williams, 1996; Sainsbury, 2000; Hall, 2001; Sinclair; 2004). While Williams refers to 'terror' she along with others refers especially to 'fear' and according to many autistic experience is very much the experience of being frightened; frightened of people, of closeness, of losing control and especially frightened of losing control over feelings.

There are professional traditions which acknowledge the importance of the autistic person's emotional life, for example 'The most striking refrain running through autistic people's accounts of their inner experience is the word "fear"' (Boucher, 1996: 87). Yet if we accept the validity of autistic insider accounts, it may seem that professional accounts do not emphasize sufficiently or represent accurately the actual experience of being autistic. Indeed it may be that we should also begin to take Jim Sinclair's advice and search for children's 'assets' rather than 'deficits' (see also Happe, 1999). However, in more self-analytical mode we might also consider whether any failure to do so might be due to our own particular emotional 'deficit': 'Thinking the unthinkable means accepting a child's knowledge of terrible experiences ... it is easier to deny the emotional reality ... than to feel the weight of their personal tragedy' (Sinason, 1992: 209, 232).

Any 'unresponsiveness' on the part of an autistic person could be seen as important scientific evidence, not necessarily of a lack of feeling/thinking but at times of their very intensity. Here are some brief examples in which I similarly speculate upon the evidence of feeling and thinking in a boy called 'James' with whom I worked for a number of years.

JAMES

From the day of our first meeting in his school, it was clear that James had some unusual ways of dealing with the world. His classteachers described him variously with words and phrases such as 'bizarre', 'he has repetitive behaviours', 'he doesn't initiate any social interaction', 'he won't give eye contact' (Billington, 2000a). It was indeed James's eyes which also held my attention and in early meetings with him he often chose to stare at objects for long periods. I wondered at the time just what he was thinking (or else avoiding) on such occasions; for example, did he stare in order to 'lose' himself in the sensory nature of the objects? Or did James stare, perhaps, to avoid looking at people: 'people do not appreciate how unbearably difficult it is for me to look at a person. It disturbs my quietness and is terribly frightening' (Jolliffe et al., 1992: 15). Many have since attested to the central role played by the sensations which are experienced, often autistic insiders, for example Temple Grandin: 'Autistic people explain [that they are] so sensitive to sound when they are young ... young children with autism may also be hypersensitive to sights, smells, tastes and tactile sensations' (Grandin and Scariano, 1996, in Boucher, 1996: 82–3).

Far from being unresponsive, therefore, it would appear there is another school of thought which suggests that autistic young people might be hypersensitive to incoming stimuli within their environment and these might overwhelm the individual's processing mechanisms. Of course it was Freud who originally pointed out that, 'protection against stimuli is an almost more important function for the living organism than reception of stimuli' (Freud, [1920] 1984: 299).

Robert Hinshelwood (1994) articulated the movement and interaction between an individual's sensations, their environmental and social context and the psychological consequences including the implications for identity when he wrote: 'The complex to-and-fro motion of the object [of our sensations] in and out of the body; the very explicit experience of concrete internal objects ... a clear link between bodily instincts and active relationships with objects' (p. 23) and even 'Identity is bound up with the introjection of objects' (p. 58).

Bion viewed the child's emerging powers of projective identification as the origins of thinking itself, as a primitive means of
dealing with the incoming (social and cultural) stimuli: 'The
activity we know as "thinking" was in origin a procedure for
unburdening the psyche of accretions of stimuli' (Bion, 1962: 31).
His 'model' of mind, therefore, suggests that thinking itself is the
activity of dealing with, or restricting the effects of, incoming
stimuli. He hypothesized that for thinking and learning to take
place we must be able to tolerate the feelings invoked by such
experiences and he suggested the consequences should those
feelings prove unbearable; 'If the learner is intolerant of the
essential frustration of learning he [sic] indulges in phantasies of
omniscience and a belief in a state where things are known'
(Bion, 1962: 65).

Bion's (1962) proposition that if we are to develop as thinkers
we need to delay the act of closure upon knowledge for as long
as possible seems especially appropriate in relation to autism. He
believed the key to all thinking was firstly, being able to process
the effects upon our feelings of sensory stimuli received and
secondly, being able to tolerate 'not knowing' for as long as
possible. In optimistic vein, there seems increasing merit in his
assertion that thinking in our species is as yet *embryonic*. More
recently, Peter Hobson has placed as central the links between a
child's affective and cognitive worlds, although he develops this
line of inquiry by emphasizing and indeed exploring in some
detail the 'close connection between what happens within an
individual person's mind and what happens between one person
and another' (Hobson, 2002: 22). Hobson thus locates the individual firmly within a social world.

Sometimes the organization of professional services prevails
against utilizing fully such complex conceptualizations when
working with children diagnosed as autistic. On such occasions
it can be difficult to resist the conclusion that a young person's
'difficulties' are mere physical phenomena lacking in human
quality, knowledge, feeling or meaning. James's use of his eyes,
however, had always seemed to me to be purposeful and I speculated that he had decided to avert his eyes as a result of a knowledge, one that may have been his acute awareness of my looking
at him as well as perhaps an anticipation of the pain that eye

contact might bring, whether physiological, psychological or both.

In work with James I reached the conclusion that the words we shared in conversation had a strong emotional component and his responses invariably suggested a connection between words used and their associated feelings. This is no mere professional hypothesis, for Donna Williams has written previously, 'Words have no meaning when the thoughts have no feelings' (Williams, 1992: 146). She went further, however, and suggested that, 'All thought begins with feeling' (p. 189).

Interestingly, one important focus of neuroscientific research is beginning to provide evidence (see Hobson, 2002, Chapter 6; Bion, 1962), which supports such hypotheses (see Damasio, 1994, 2000, 2004). Interesting also is how the person with the disability (in this case, autism) when allowed a 'voice' may access insightful truths which are in advance of professional knowledge.

I would argue, therefore, that James and many other young people who have been consigned to a disempowering category can have human capacities for thinking and feeling which are often poorly represented by the language of an individualized psychopathology and the conventional models of deficit which underpin many professional and service practices.

SYMBOLS AND FRIENDS

In Donna Williams's autobiography she describes how certain people she had met assumed another life inside her and became symbols and even aspects of her personality which were necessary for her to survive in the world. Psychodynamic approaches have provided a basis upon which to theorize such phenomena:

> the manifold aims of different types of projective identification, for example, splitting off and getting rid of unwanted parts of the self into an object to dominate and control it and thus avoid any feelings of being separate. Thus the infant, or adult, who goes on using such mechanisms powerfully can avoid any awareness of any separateness, dependence, admiration, or its concomitant sense of loss, anger, envy, and so on. (Joseph, 1988: 168–9)

James seemed to people his world with 'friends' in ways which resemble some of the types of projective identification above. In response to one question during an early session, "Who are your friends?" James began to 'drift off' (see Alvarez, 1992). When at length I structured for him a possible response which allowed him to be both positive and at the same time preserve his defences (and his friends perhaps) intact, he chose to re-engage with me. Indeed given the opportunity to initiate or control interaction, again in such a way as to leave his defences intact, James eventually asked me a question, "how many friends have you?"

This seemed no mere reframing of my first question, which had been delivered without any great intelligence on my part. Indeed James's initial responses to my questions about friends, together with his own question to me, seemed to contain a profound intelligence for which I was ill-prepared and to which I was initially ill-inclined. Valerie Sinason again points to the possibility that adults and professionals might have difficulty in acknowledging the thinking or knowing of such children, which is our own deficit; she refers to 'The disbelief ... in trying ... to consider the child's intelligence' (Sinason, 1992: 209). In contrast, James's question to me might suggest a conceptual preoccupation with one of life's great questions, considered at some length and articulated by Aristotle as, 'How many friends should you have?' (Aristotle, 1976: 307).

During the excellent work conducted by his adult teaching assistant in school, James sometimes began to reveal his own world of imaginary friends. He seemed to retreat to these friends at moments of danger, or perhaps even boredom – another state of mind which might itself hold perils for him. At what point does such mental activity become pathological, however, as opposed to necessary, creative, imaginative or even pleasurable?

A year or so after the initial meeting with him, I visited James and his parents at their home and at the end of the evening he introduced me to another aspect of his friends. I had spent an hour or so talking with his parents, amongst other things asking for their permission to include James and themselves in my research. James did not look directly at any of us during this time but I found myself thinking that he was processing every word that was spoken as he sat on the floor playing (with a 400 piece jigsaw) and without saying a word (James was noisy, 'hyperactive' and highly disruptive in class and ADHD had been a first diagnostic consideration).

As I was leaving James suddenly spoke and asked me, 'would you like to see my things?' He took me upstairs and on the landing at the top of the stairs he showed me a huge, old chest of drawers. Only with an immense effort did he open one of the great drawers, crammed full to overflowing with books. Clearly, these books which he was proudly introducing were the 'things' and were significant. His identification with the objects seemed so strong that I even wondered whether these were not just his things but his 'friends'; I thus immediately became alive to the importance and privilege of the moment. I hoped that James could sense my interpretation and understanding of the value of the symbolic life which the books held for him, but the moment assumed a different quality, however, when he then asked of me, "how many things have you?"

The question almost paralyzed me as I became even more aware of the importance of what was taking place and my intelligence, my own thinking/feeling had to stir in response to his. For James's 'friends' and/or 'things', I hypothesized, played a crucial role in his attempts to connect 'his world' with 'the world' outside of him. I speculated further that his friends might not only be his means of mediating or perhaps controlling the world, but might also offer a potential means of communicating.

The importance of the moment which I had sensed as James pulled open the drawer could well have been a realization of the communicative nature of James's act. For he was not merely initiating social interaction, he was communicating with me in the fullest, perhaps even purest, form. He was showing me his world and placing it in me. It would be vital within this truly interactionist paradigm, therefore, to offer his world back to him undamaged. The truly communicative act on James's part, however, was that in asking of me "how many things have you?" he was inviting me to place part of my world back into him. This was spontaneous, communicative and reciprocal.

The cause of my paralysis was connected to amazement once again at the bravery of James's act, for indeed, there could well have been dangers for him in lowering his defences so completely. Yet this risk could be a necessary leap for us all if we are ever to connect ourselves to the world outside, to other 'friends' and 'things': 'when every separation is experienced as annihilation, all the child can do is construct for himself (sic) a world in which he tries hard to live without affects in order to keep himself safe from the threat of destruction' (Mannoni, 1999).

PROFESSIONAL PRACTICES

So what do we do as professionals when we are working with an autistic child? Several years ago now Donna Williams provided some advice.

> What I liked (about teacher) ... was that there were no wrong answers. (Williams, 1992: 42)
>
> My father had all the right responses; he simply sat within my presence, letting me show him how I felt in the only way I could – via objects. (ibid: 67)
>
> I had reached out to Mary (psychiatrist) as somebody I could 'trust' in the world. She had accepted me as more than a patient; she had accepted me personally. (ibid: 108)
>
> Bryn (friend) would simply come and exist in my company. (ibid: 121)

In a professional world of 'targets', 'strategies', and other manic 'doing', the value of physical inactivity is lost. The social contexts and processes to which James and perhaps many others can be subjected often do not provide such space, but instead surround a young person with lifeless artefacts – unfeeling strategies, stripped of meaning, that have little concern for the subtle and qualitative nature of meaningful human interaction, communication or experience.

In order to act ethically in the field of autism, therefore, it is necessary to hold on to fundamental human issues – of feeling, thinking and meaning. Before this can happen practitioners have to overcome our own deficit and begin to contemplate not just autistic defences but also our own feelings and defences. We might come to tolerate our own frustration as a prompt for our own (social) thinking and learning. Such bravery may be required on our part if we are to avoid constructing policies, services and professional practices that only mirror an autistic tendency to construct defences against unpleasurable or painful experiences.

The difficulty faced by an autistic child, therefore, lies not solely within themselves but in those around them; but how able are we to provide services and practices that are sensitive to these issues? How able are we to provide modes of interaction or communication or the silent presence especially when we might not be able to tolerate our own fears or quest for meaning? Certainly current services can lack the sensitivity suggested by Jordan et al. (DfEE, 1998a).

The consequences for the autistic child should we fail to provide sensitive responses are considerable. If we are unable to tolerate our own human profundity (or lack of), we are destined to leave the autistic child also in a state of isolation. While the problems for an autistic child can be exacerbated by the people and objects within their environment the argument here, supported by the theoretical possibilities outlined above, surely begs the more hopeful hypothesis that whether as professionals or as family members we can play a crucial role. For it suggests that there are approaches we can adopt and ways we can 'be' that might alleviate some aspects of autistic isolation.

FINAL THOUGHTS

There are many theories in existence now which if utilized can lead to more sophisticated professional practices, for example ideas about theory of mind (Baron-Cohen et al., 1993), central coherence (Frith, 1989), executive function, sensory integration (Kranowitz, 1998) and meaningful perception (Durig, 1996). Rather than lamely adhering merely to the mechanistic traits of diagnostic criteria, therefore, I suggest that the challenge for service providers, policy makers and practitioners is to:

- attempt to conceive something of the immensity of the human quest for meaning, mind and consciousness which is raised by consideration of autism;
- develop professional/assessment practices and also new ways of talking about autism that concentrate on assets rather than deficits;
- endeavour to create services that can act more effectively as 'containers' (Bion, 1970) for difficult feelings/distress;

- continue to seek interventions that are sensitive to interactionist possibilities and that avoid isolating the child by placing responsibilities for behavioural change not just upon the child but upon us adults – as parents and professionals;
- develop approaches which help to preserve rather than deny the real within our own experience;
- support those who realize fully the importance and the value of the work we can do with individual autistic children;
- search more vigorously for ways in which we can access the views of autistic children in order to identify how they currently manage their 'worlds'.

The daily dilemmas posed by social circumstances which are inherently individualizing demand decisions based upon the advice which we might give and those strategies we must choose at the individual level. Paradoxically, however, we might connect with autistic young people and their ability to develop and learn not just by focusing upon those individuals, but by keeping alive the vitality of our own experience and by acknowledging our own experiential lives in work with them.

Autism somehow seems to demand that we consider the boundaries between physiological and psychological experiences, not least our own. The challenge ultimately is to find ways in which we can provide services that are designed not only to meet the material needs of adults (parents and professionals), but also those that will encourage the experiential well-being of young people.

FURTHER READING

Billington, T. (2000a) *Separating, Losing and Excluding Children: Narratives of difference*. London: Routledge Falmer.

Billington, T., McNally, B. and McNally, C. (2000) Autism: working with parents and discourse in experience, expertise and learning. *Educational Psychology in Practice*, 16 (1): 59–68.

Boucher, J. (1996). 'The inner life of children with autistic difficulties', in V. Varma (ed.), *The Inner Life of Children with Special Educational Needs*. London: Whurr.

Hobson, P. (2002) *The Cradle of Thought: Exploring the origins of thinking*. London: Sage.

Reflexive Activity

What are the practical and ethical issues raised when trying to construct narratives of experience relating to an autistic young person? Reflect on how or indeed whether those issues should be overcome. Note down some of the consequences for the young person should they not be able to control the direction of their own chosen narrative.

9 NARRATIVE SCIENCE

The chief characteristic of the specifically human life ... is that it is always full of events which ultimately can be told as a story ... (Arendt, 1958: 72)

The apparent contradiction inherent within the term 'narrative science' may be difficult for some to resolve. At one extreme there could be those among you who have been immersed in one of the natural sciences and who would regard all aspirations or claims made by any of the social sciences to be real science to be deeply flawed and at the very least inferior in their claims to truth. Then there will be those social scientists engaged in what they regard as scientific research (which for the last hundred years has tended to mean 'experiments' which produce 'results' and which lead to conclusions as 'facts'); they may regard with some skepticism claims by any practitioner that they work according to the scientific method, for example those working with children, since theoretical or 'academic' knowledge can be regarded as superior to knowledge acquired through practice (this is related to the primacy of the 'cognitive' discussed in Chapter 6).

However, I shall present another possibility here and one already voiced in Chapter 2 that the current, 'dominant' conception of a science is itself only in its infancy within the broad sweep of human history. There are more ancient understandings, indeed the word 'science' found its way into English from the Latin 'scientia' meaning 'knowledge'. That knowledge should be the sole preserve of only one very particular kind of human endeavour (that obtained through some narrowly-conceived procedures of experimental methodology) is clearly a bold position to take, exemplified in the following definition of science as '... those branches of study that apply scientific method to the phenomena of the physical universe ...' (*Shorter Oxford English Dictionary*, 2002).

But older uses do persist which perhaps become more relevant in social research, for example the alternative meaning that science is 'the state of fact or knowing: knowledge or cognizance of something specified or implied ...' (*Shorter Oxford English Dictionary* 2002). In this chapter, I use the word 'science' in order to preserve another older and traditional usage which defines science as 'knowledge acquired by study: acquaintance with or mastery of a department of learning ... skilful technique ... a craft, trade, or occupation requiring trained skill ...' (*Shorter Oxford English Dictionary*, 2002). I would suggest that this understanding has the potential to make the concept of science less remote and a more accessible, dare I say more inclusive, socially-situated practice.

Those of us who have engaged in the systematic study of young people or who have been trained to work with children will be aware of different theories or practices which have come to define our respective disciplines. For example, as social workers you may have been encouraged to see the child according to a range of social situations or as a member of a particular social group and you might have developed a specialist knowledge in respect of specific issues such as disability, gender or ethnicity (variables). You may also have developed therapeutic skills, although increasingly there is a perception at least that the scope for such intense individual work seems to be reducing. The knowledge possessed by social workers, however, has at times been undermined not only by the status of their work as mere practice but also I would suggest by the way that the discipline has not sought to identify itself only as a science rooted in the experimental method. In particular, sociology (and thereafter social work) has not permitted itself to be dominated solely by the results of quantitative data.

In British education the notion of a discrete pedagogical science has struggled to survive and many new teachers entering the profession might be left with little alternative but to view their primary role in practice as that of leading their cohorts to the achievement of particular test measures in accordance with governmental targets. In contrast to such narrow conceptions, meanwhile, many of us might be able to testify from personal experience of schooling to the impact upon our lives made by the sheer commitment and dedication of individual teachers who have been prepared to offer more to us than simple comments upon our progress or our inclination to learn. Indeed, teachers have been and continue to be uniquely positioned to participate in children's lives in a very special way, engaged as they are in prolonged daily contact with their protégés. Under such conditions more comprehensive and lasting 'relationships' can be seen to develop, although as the pressures to adopt a distanced professionalism increase so teachers' positions as community practitioners come under threat.

Psychologists working with children, while divided by professional training in recent decades into 'clinical' and 'educational', have also differed in their efforts to work according to the dictates of the 'scientific method'. Psychologists from both branches can each be divided further into those who are inclined to base their work on a diagnostic model on the one hand and those who seek qualitatively based explanations on the other.

It is not my intention here to recommend the supremacy of one particular branch of knowledge making or practice over another, however, for such an enterprise would probably leave many of the underlying processes intact. Certainly, there is much merit in a branch of science which merely seeks to deny the null hypothesis, but there could be criticisms that the discourses and practices built on this model too easily slide into assumptions of truth. Qualitative research methods are often used for emancipatory purposes (not least in this book) although I would say that quantitative research also possesses such potentials. Indeed it is legitimate but also important to know the extent of situations which are thought to be problematic. It is clearly useful to have information which allows us to consider the extent of dangerous situations, one such example being that out of over 250 young people in a Scottish secondary school 'over 32% wrote that they were currently witnessing domestic abuse' (Alexander et al., 2005: 187).

Null hypothesis

'... a basic rule of experimental research. If there is no possibility that an experiment might go *against* the experimental hypothesis, then there is no point in doing the experiment at all. Consequently, an experimental hypothesis is always tested against a *null hypothesis*, which states that an experimenter will *not* find the experimental results he or she expects.' (Greene and D'Oliveira, 1982: 8)

Such results could and indeed should affect the nature of professional services offered to young people and practitioners need to be conversant with both the techniques and the value of such practices. While we need to be able to analyse and contextualize such data, however, it is important that we have the critical acumen which allows us to scrutinize such processes from different positions; not least because practitioners have other responsibilities. While we might choose to work out the effects of such phenomena in our communities and look to provide systems of support, we also need to be able to see where the very organization of services can exacerbate situations or difficulties, for example in a too simplistic adherence to a diagnostic model. We need to be able to work sometimes with young people on an individual basis and on such occasions we will need to perform our work in ways which do not compound any harmful effect. Warner (forthcoming) provides one useful starting point by articulating the need in her work with abused young people to make explicit to them her difference from the other adults in their lives, to 'signal my difference from abusers ... (by being) clear and transparent regarding what I am and why I am here' (Warner, forthcoming).

We return again then to the questions posed earlier as to how we should work with, speak with and listen to young people, especially when the models of human behaviour to which they may have previously been subjected may not have been afforded to conditions of such safety or freedom of expression. The need for young people to be safe is a discourse which has perhaps never before been so widely circulated or accepted in families, schools or communities. It is particularly incumbent on professionals working with children to ensure that our own practices do not constitute threats in any way to the well-being of a young person, although ensuring the paramountcy of the welfare of the child can be difficult always to sustain.

NARRATIVES IN PRACTICE

Where children are able to talk openly about the processes of change that affect their lives they are more likely to develop coping strategies themselves. This has been seen as a major contributor to resilience in childhood. (Dowling and Barnes, 2000: 67)

The ability to communicate via a language which is spontaneous and imaginative can be regarded as the unique characteristic of human being and the work we conduct with children is to a large extent dependent on our ability to engage with them, in particular through the exchange of language. From Freud onwards, negotiations between professional and client have been conducted according to the parameters set by language, although not exclusively so.

The kind of conversations enjoyed (or otherwise) by professionals and their clients have traditionally been determined according to the laws of a power relationship in which one participant (the professional) has often dictated the content, scope and direction of the interaction. Once invited into a situation the professional might have questions to ask or tests to conduct and the child will be assessed and judged according to their responses. This situation would seem still to exist as children across the age range are the subjects and recipients of adult assessment practices on a number of issues which are invariably connected in some way either to their development, their well-being or education. In particular, it is frequently the behaviour of young people or their ability to learn which demands our adult attention and which operates usually according to discourses of children as incompetent adults. The 1989 Children Act, however, did make explicit the position of the child as 'victim' in relation to deviant adults and perhaps as never before the position of children in relation to adults was changed in law.

It is not the argument here that assessment of children should cease for there are compelling arguments to suggest that our young people continue to be in need of protection from us, especially when it is becoming apparent that many children still suffer in silence at the hands of adult abusers (DoH, 1995). It is the case, however, that some professional concepts and practices can be rather better than others in permitting sensitive engagement with young people regarding those issues which are of concern to them:

> ... narrative research respects each individual story and whatever shape of life that emerges from a person's account of times of uncertainty and fixity ... this sense of personal identity emerges as 'figure' against the 'ground' of culturally given images of the self ... identity operates as a complement to and consolation for alienation. (Parker, 2005: 72)

During the last twenty years an increasing number of practitioners and researchers have been employing narrative approaches in their work, not merely to accord with personal values (primarily social or political) but actually in many respects to accord with the principles of science-practitioner, for access to data in the form of young people's accounts can illuminate and thus inform practice. We seem to be in an autobiographical age but narrative work, whilst concentrating on individual accounts, should not be confused with a notion of mere story-telling as entertainment. Narratives can take many forms (see Genette, 1980; Hollway, 1989; and Billington, 2000a, for analysis of this point) but in work with children narrative practice is designed primarily to address the needs of the young person in order that they develop a knowledge of themselves which only they can possess. While such work might invoke a range of emotions, including sadness or happiness, it might also deal with the tragic or profound (or even mundane) but always the space created will be an opportunity for the young person to access some form of truth about themselves.

In Chapter 8 the reader was invited to consider the ways in which autistic 'insiders', for example, might provide us with vital insights into their particular ways of living and being in the world. It was suggested that their evidence might be invaluable in ensuring that we meet their needs if only *we* could begin to achieve more sophisticated approaches to understanding and communication.

However, in the case of James it was not only the words that he spoke which were significant but the totality of the situation in which he interacted with me. We need to be aware that while 'Practitioners and researchers have made progress, in recent years, in seeking the views of children and young people less progress has been made in seeking the views of young people with significant communication and/or cognitive impairments [sic] ...' (Morris, 2003: 337).

Indeed my ability to conceptualize narratives not merely through words but once again through the totality of social exchange has proved necessary not just in the case of Michael (Chapter 4), but in work with a host of other young people who are commonly regarded as disabled. For example, one young boy called 'David' (Billington et al., 2000) could shut down his sensory antennae so effectively to a cacophony of sounds, sights and smells in his classroom that he often presented as blind and deaf. And yet in his endlessly repeated movements around the class it became clear that he was physically capable of seeing and hearing. The more I stood motionless and watched him the more it became possible to see the extent to which this was self-defence, by protecting himself from the vast array of sensory stimuli with which others in the class were dealing routinely. But David did not quite obliterate all stimuli, since when I replicated exactly a sound he habitually made with a small toy it prompted a sudden turn of his head in my direction despite the almost overwhelming noise around him.

David's movements in class were fascinating as the pattern of his trajectory across the room was replicated constantly and with precision. He seemed to be mapping or even constructing the limits of his perceptual field, yet while apparently not seeing anything around him he would step over or avoid any obstruction in his chosen route without looking and without faltering. In arriving at my opinion I had to combine a 'knowledge' acquired through study (for example, during training or else through access to research on autism, human communication and development) with a different kind of knowledge which was capable of responding to the very specific human circumstances in which the phenomena were being observed.

To view David as mere 'phenomena', however, seems antithetical to the professional stance which I still seek, for regarding him merely as interesting phenomena or indeed as a set of behaviours as opposed primarily to his human being surely spells danger for a science-practitioner committed to ethical practice. David could not apparently be accessed through words and so conceiving of his needs required an imaginative leap from practitioners although this will always be subject to ethical restrictions. The development of a narrative science (as methodology), therefore, demands that we work not only according to the social requirements and responsibilities of our particular professional position but also that we remember the inter-personal obligations demanded in a civilized society.

I believe this requires us to achieve a fundamental change in our approach to disability in all its forms, for in assessing David it could be argued that my disability could contribute to his should I fail to make that imaginative leap.

PRINCIPLES OF NARRATIVE PRACTICE

People attempt to make sense of their lives by narrativising their experiences (see for example Kearney, 2002); they tell stories, both to others and to themselves, not merely through words but through actions. In the rest of this chapter, however, I shall consider ways in which narrative practices can be utilized, primarily through the use of spoken language.

As I indicated earlier, there are some crucial 'distinctions' to bear in mind when working with children through language-use. Firstly, there is the dilemma that adult accounts can be different from those accounts that a young person might choose to express themselves. This was specifically considered in Chapter 8, for example in respect of young people diagnosed as autistic; such analysis can be related to many other circumstances and in respect of any diagnosis, where the application occurred without the consent or full knowledge of the recipient. For example in his therapeutic work with 'Paul', a boy previously diagnosed, Ian Law suggests that through analysis of their conversations it '... can be seen from the transcript, the question of whether ADD [Attention Deficit Disorder] "exists" or not was an irrelevance, as it completely failed to engage [Paul]. It was more experience that had been applied to him' (Law, 1997: 296).

The fracture between a merely professional knowledge and a young person's experience thus becomes apparent once more, a dilemma articulated finely elsewhere as 'there is an abyss between knowledge and experience that cannot be bridged scientifically' (Damasio, 2000: 307–8). There are difficulties, therefore, in being able to exchange language in ways which are able to represent the meaning and the nature of individual experience and as stated earlier this can be compounded by a host of other issues, many of which stumble at the hurdle of the imperfect nature of communication in human relations (Lacan, 1977).

Perhaps most controversially, if we do actually build our professional practices upon people's accounts can we believe what they tell us? In the context of this book, to what extent can we believe what children tell us? Research evidence does exist relating to children and lies obtained through empirical research, mainly in respect of children within the court system, but while there would appear to be some significant age variables there can be no simple conclusion that children are less reliable in testimony than adults (see for example Waterman et al., 1995). Nevertheless, there are dangers in relying solely on narrative accounts which can be put succinctly as follows:

> Will you believe everything you are told? If not, how will you distinguish between truth and untruth? Even if you believe everything you are told, will you be satisfied that you have been told everything that is relevant? How would you define this, and how would you know? What do you assume about the effect of people's motivations and memory on what they tell you? What will you assume about your effect as interviewer on the answers given? Does your sex, race, age and so on make a difference? (Hollway and Jefferson, 2000: 2)

A narrative practice which is incapable of tolerating the problems, ambiguities or uncertainties of language, therefore, runs the risk of developing practices which are either unscientific or at worst actually dangerous in their consequences for the individual recipient of professional practice.

> In everyday informal dealings with each other, we do not take each other's accounts at face value, unless we are totally naïve; we question, disagree, bring in counter-examples, interpret, notice hidden agendas. (Hollway and Jefferson, 2000: 3)

So not only do we have the problem spelt out by Damasio that there is a distinction between knowledge and experience, but there is also a potential problem in the words that people use to account for their experience. For there is a risk in work with children that the words we use may not merely fail to engage (Law, 1997) but might more proactively 'operate to separate people from their experiences by purloining accounts of their lives and by laying claim to greater knowledge and truth' (Billington, 2000a: 36). There is a need, therefore, to pursue the development of practices which are emancipatory in that they look to reduce and not exacerbate the effects of any difference.

The risk is that for young people such as Michael, David or James, the professional might fail to engage; furthermore professionals cannot be immune to the often competing demands of professional knowledge and experience. Any clumsy account of a disabled-ness might not merely constitute a failure to engage, therefore, but may eventually change the ways in which a young person views themselves. In fact we may serve to convince a young person of their 'problem'. The upshot of professional services for a young woman called 'Mary' with whom I worked in a previous study were serious for it was difficult to avoid concluding in the very way just suggested that she 'had become separated from her own history – by the weight of numerous professionalized and institutionalized re-readings' (2000a: 37).

So notwithstanding the aforementioned difficulties and most legitimate critical concerns there are principles of working with children according to narrative methodologies that seek to engage, but in the process make a conscious effort to avoid superimposing yet another adult-preferred account. In order to avoid these dangers, certain practices are recommended by narrative practitioners and researchers: 'Always maintaining a stance of curiosity ... Always asking questions to which you genuinely do not know the answers' (Morgan, 2000: 1) but also – '[the] responsibility is to be a good listener and the interviewee is a story-teller rather than a respondent' (Hollway and Jefferson, 2000: 53).

Some practitioners have developed such principles into specific and sophisticated techniques. For example Michael White and David Epston, whose backgrounds were in family therapy, have been particularly active in searching for practices which not only address directly the issue of the adult-child power relationship but which allow the young person some space to tell of their own 'preferred story'.

The concepts these authors develop, of 'externalizing the problem', 'relative influence questioning' (or 'mapping the influence of the problem', 'mapping the influence of the persons') and 'unique outcomes' (whether 'historical', 'present' or 'future') are examples of specific techniques. The authors claim their methods open up 'new possibilities for (young people) to describe themselves, each other, and their relationships from a new, non problem- saturated perspective; ... [enable] the development of an alternative story' (White and Epston, 1990: 39). They also claim that narrative therapy results in:

- a decrease in unproductive conflict, for example disputes over who is responsible for the problem;
- undermining the sense of failure;
- co-operation in struggling against the problem;
- the opening up of new possibilities to take action against the problem and its influence;

- a lighter, less stressed approach;
- options for dialogue rather than monologue. (White and Epston, 1990: 41)

These would indeed seem to be desirable outcomes when working with young people but other authors/practitioners have perhaps been more cautious in their claims and it is possible to reach other conceptual conclusions, for example Wendy Hollway identifies the following as crucial in her approach:

> the biographical-interpretative method and its four interviewing principles designed to facilitate the production of interviewees' meaning-frames (or gestalts), namely: use open questions, elicit stories, avoid 'why' questions and follow respondents' ordering and phrasing. (Hollway and Jefferson, 2000: 3)

There are other practitioners who have been working according to similar principles which have been known for many years now (see Kelly, 1955; Dowling and Osborne, 1985; Dowling and Barnes; 2000). Increasingly, well-refined means of developing narrative practices (both clinical and research) based on the principle of social engagement or a contract are becoming more widely available. How do we construct different kinds of relationships with young people in practice, therefore, and can such practices be incorporated in the assessments which are required by statutory agencies – or indeed should they be? The following examples are taken from my work in Children Act assessments conducted for courts in England and Wales.

NARRATIVE ASSESSMENTS

Working upon the principle that 'assessments are interventions' demands that those of us who assess children in whatever domain analyse not only the situation surrounding a child, but the impact our work has upon them. It is always necessary to assume both a position and the analytical mode in which we are placed as a participant. Indeed any assessment conducted by any professional from across the children's workforce, whether in education, health or social care, constitutes an intervention in a young person's life. Only in a tiny minority of cases can such assessment arise naturally from within the young person's usual, chosen, social orbit and indeed, I can recall only a handful of occasions when I was approached directly by a young person to intervene in their lives. Assessments are almost always within the gift and control of adults at the current time and the purposes can if we are not careful be determined largely by adult needs, or at least in respect of a child's needs as defined by an adult. Once again the aim is not to argue against such assessments, for many of these interventions will be necessary under current social conditions in ensuring the adequate protection and acceptable development of our young people in accord with current beliefs and values.

One important belief/value that has emerged during the last decade or so following ratification of the UN Convention on Children's Rights is the importance of allowing the young person to have a 'voice' in matters relating to the decision-making processes in their lives. Narrative approaches conducted by professionals are ideally suited in attending to this principle. Just as I provided Luke space to play with ideas about his family (Chapters 4 and 7), James space to play with ideas about his 'friends' or things' (Chapter 8) or indeed chose not to invade Michael's space (Chapter 4), it has been an important approach to assessment that a young person is allowed this significant space in which to develop ways of thinking and feeling about themselves and/or their situation. There are similarities here with the pedagogical methods espoused by Vygotsky ('zone of proximal development', 1978) and Bruner ('scaffolding'; Wood et al., 1976) and also Bion's (1962 and 1970) understanding of the interconnectivity of learning and feeling, as well as his concept of containment. Each of these theories has proved to be an important resource which has directly affected practice. An important additional principle, however, is that the potential space between the child and the professional should be one in which both participants can enter or depart with basic safety assured (see Winnicott, 1971).

Wendy Hollway quite rightly posed a dilemma when she questioned our inclination to believe everything we are told. However, there can be other occasions when even a very young child is able to provide insights into their own situation which are either 'beyond their years' or else are essential in formulating opinion. The dilemmas relating to narrative practice and truth, therefore, are many and complex.

'Melanie' was in her infant school when she suffered the loss of her mother in tragic circumstances. The particular context of events involving family members was such that the court clearly had good reason to be concerned about Melanie and her well-being in the future. There were questions to be answered in respect of her current need for 'therapy', her future needs in respect of her social and emotional development and not least questions relating to her contact with particular family members. Utilizing again the concept of children's material 'spaces' (see James et al., 1998: Chapter 2), the evidence from other close family members at home was that while she had been unsettled for a while Melanie had adjusted really well to her new situation and was behaving, sleeping and eating normally. I was told that there were no problems in the local community and that she was playing with her friends and adjusting well to her new school.

I accessed additional information which corroborated this position and spoke with other professionals including teachers in school. Remarkably, Melanie did in fact seem to be getting on with life despite her experiences, all the changes in her life and clearly, not least, despite the loss of her mother. Given the specific instructions from the court, however, which were issued with good reason in the interests of ensuring safety, it was necessary to see to what extent this situation could be corroborated as broadly positive by Melanie herself. Assessing a child's emotional well-being and accessing their wishes can be especially difficult when consideration of such matters might in itself demand that the young person has to re-visit particular memories of events or feelings which one might assume to be distressing. Just as the imposition of a category might be unwanted by a young person, so too might they wish to avoid confronting difficult or potentially traumatic memories.

Once again projective techniques can be helpful for whilst not scientific in the sense of being easily generalizable to all other 'similar' situations, they are scientific in their ability to provide insights and knowledge in a manner which frequently allows participants more safely to contain the effects of any issues raised (both for the client and the professional). The Bene-Anthony Test (1957) allowed Melanie to introduce her mother into our session in a way chosen by her. During its performance she was also able to show her affection for her mother above all other family members and she began to tell me about what she used to enjoy doing with her and what she missed in her life now.

Melanie also told me about the positive feelings she had for various other family members and although still only at infant school, she was quite able to provide me with a reasoned, coherent account of her life at that present time. The manner in which she expressed her wishes in respect of specific issues was congruent with the overall rationale of her narrative. At one point she even introduced a highly sensitive issue into her account, but while she volunteered some information she then reflected and in a calm manner which was not in the least capricious she added "but I don't want to talk about it." She had used the safe space provided and created her own boundary. In this case I deemed Melanie's responses in our exchange to be encouraging.

Clearly, if we are to respect the thrust of recent legislation relating to children's rights the views of children such as Melanie should be sought and respected. I would suggest in such work that the onus of proof should fall upon us as adult professionals to justify why we should not accede to a child's wishes, either sought or freely expressed. While Melanie had provided mature insights at the age of six years, the virulence of these aforementioned discourses of 'ability' (see Chapter 3) and the child as 'incompetent' adult is such that there can always be a temptation to rely on psychometric tests as a means of ascertaining an age-equivalence figure in order to reassure the court. Indeed in order to lend weight to my argument I did conduct some tests with Melanie, the results of which enabled me to suggest positively on her behalf that she seemed to be under-achieving in respect of her school attainments. However, I did not need psychometric data to confirm Melanie's intelligence or authenticity. Knowledge of this arose from different kinds of understanding more related to imaginative hypothesis – formation and an ability to tolerate a myriad of variables.

A further (not-so-hidden) agenda here, however, was that I was searching for Melanie's strengths in accord with the principle that it is necessary for those working with children to 'make an explicit commitment to detailing people's strengths. This does not mean avoid problems, but situate them' (Warner, forthcoming). Clearly, however, while mobilizing a range of issues to meet Melanie's needs in accord with her own wishes, it was not possible to ignore or eradicate that tenacious discourse of ability which, of course, while serving a positive effect on this occasion could lead equally to more negative consequences (for example disenfranchisement should the young person be deemed not fit to give evidence, or in other circumstances as a means of exclusion from or removal to another school).

Irrespective of Melanie's results in psychometric tests, I did not need any convincing of the good sense of her views. Just as it can be scientifically erroneous to assume that children tell more lies than adults, child development accounts which employ a simple competence model in which adults 'can' and young people 'can't' do not always serve us well. Melanie was truly remarkable with many fine qualities and potentials to which many of us as adults could not easily aspire. But she would not present as so remarkable in quite the same way if we were accustomed in daily practice to searching for such strengths and qualities whenever we worked with children. Indeed Melanie's abilities in coping with extremes of experience could begin to seem almost 'normal', supported as she was by family, friends and teachers.

There will be many of us who could cite cases in which a young person has been able to make significant contributions to their own assessments, whose wishes are deemed reasonable and acceptable in ways with which they might not previously have been thought capable. Particular problems can arise, however, when a young person's views and wishes run counter to those of a parent or a carer or indeed our own.

MAKING A CHOICE: WHEN PARENTS AND YOUNG PEOPLE DISAGREE

In respect of 'Rebecca', her early years had been marked by parental strife and a family history of mental health issues together with substance abuse and chaotic living conditions. Practitioner experience as well as results from research led us quite reasonably to conclude a likelihood that under these circumstances Rebecca would be in danger of suffering harm (see for example Dixon et al., 2005a; Dixon et al., 2005b).

She was thus removed from her parents and placed in foster care with carers who after several years wished to adopt her. To all intents and purposes Rebecca would seem to have flourished in her new situation, especially in terms of her physical health but also in respect of her general development – social, emotional and educational. While one of her biological parents supported the local authority's proposal, however, the other parent objected and even expressed a wish to assume care for Rebecca.

As always, the issues in this case were both numerous and complex and were not all related to psychological functioning but also to education and health matters. There were also other concerns which would lend themselves undoubtedly to sociological explanations whilst economic and even political arguments were invoked during proceedings. Once again, I attempted to access all available documentation and sources of evidence, meeting the various parties and protagonists in order to create a comprehensive map of Rebecca's life, past and present. This perhaps marks an extreme case of what I referred to earlier as the 'intensive scrutiny' that can be directed towards a child's life and we should be vigilant in ensuring such invasion can be justified as being in their 'best interests'.

Rebecca too was fed up of all the investigations and she told me this in no uncertain terms when we first met. She was clearly not in the mood for an overly-sensitive approach on my part in which I would extract information in as gentle a manner as was possible. She knew what she wanted and her mind was made up. She even took it upon herself to write for me a letter which she wished to be given to the judge and which told him exactly what she thought the decision of the court should be.

So, should the professional merely accept her view and act accordingly or are there other considerations? Well clearly the adversarial nature of the legal system in England and Wales allows such a position (especially one expressed by a minor) to be challenged, not least since the parent wishing to assume custody was in disagreement with their own daughter. Here the parent believed that not only did Rebecca not really hold such views, but on the contrary that she did in fact really want to leave her current carers; thus she was merely expressing views not only as a result of the pressure she was under from the said carers but also from many of the professionals involved.

There was previous evidence that Rebecca had on occasion presented differently according to circumstance, so was she merely confused or did she have one 'real' view which could be accessed as the basis for providing opinion? Once again hypothesis-formation (Piontelli, 1992), delaying the foreclosure upon knowledge as 'fact' (Bion, 1962) and the ability to contextualize any knowledge (Warner, forthcoming; see also 'social framework evidence', Raitt and Zeedyk, 2000), while not in themselves theories and practices which expedite matters quickly, were vital in arriving eventually at an opinion.

I have already stated that the professional should assume responsibility for providing the burden of proof should they not wish to accept the view of a young person. In this case, Rebecca gave me no direct evidence in her own accounts to me which allowed me to dismiss her view. But there was some evidence provided by the parent seeking custody who supplied some letters from Rebecca which were full of expressions of love, warmth and loss. Yet to me (and others) Rebecca remained absolutely consistent in expressing a wish to be adopted by her current carers.

Contact with the parent in question had ceased for several months on account of that person's overt hostility to social workers and a refusal to observe contact rules and conditions. However, Rebecca continued to have rewarding contact with the other parent who seemed also to be the most significant attachment figure in her life, although she knew and had long since accepted that this parent could not care for her. Rebecca meanwhile continued as ever to be adamant about the inability of her other parent to care for her.

The hypothesis that Rebecca had become accustomed to taking responsibility for her parents in a psychological sense seemed increasingly tenable. Given the general manner of the parent seeking custody I was fearful lest she be overwhelmed during any clumsy attempt to reinstate some form of contact between them (while some interpreted this particular parent's behaviour as threatening I deemed it not to be calculatingly so, but more a reflection of their own uncontainable needs). So as a first step I suggested this parent should write to Rebecca and that she could then reply. Since I was once again concerned about Rebecca's vulnerability to emotional states (in particular, those of her parents) I also suggested that I could help the parent construct a letter which might be helpful to her.

Rebecca's joy at receipt of this letter was such that she replied immediately and once again in a most affectionate manner. Significantly, however, she replied in a way which maintained the safe boundaries of exchange that I had hypothesized she sought. Her response seemed to me to have qualities which could be analysed according to the principles of closeness-distance described previously (see Chapter 2 and also Wilkinson, 1993). While Rebecca was happy to express warm feelings of affection in respect of both her parents, she had become accustomed to the safety of having control over the ways in which such feelings and related interactions were exchanged and conducted. Unfortunately the parent seeking custody was unable to sustain this measured approach and as far as could be ascertained wished not only to assume contact with Rebecca, but to have the right to modes of exchange with her in which I feared again that she would be overwhelmed by the sheer force of emotional states likely to be thrust upon her.

Rebecca thus held firm to her wishes of not wanting to live with either parent, but also not even to have contact with the parent seeking custody until conditions of safety could be assured. Rejecting her views could not be supported by evidence. Once again while I accepted her wishes and indeed had done so immediately the arguments to support her position were only amassed by a careful, even painstaking, acquisition of data from a range of sources. Rebecca meanwhile had herself spent years pouring over this same data and I suspect now that in those robust and concise opening comments to me at our very first meeting there was a dense weight of analysis. All my professional endeavours, therefore, had eventually merely arrived at Rebecca's own self-assessment which had clearly been based on the evidence of years of experience.

What are the issues though, if we disagree with the child's wishes?

FURTHER READING

Dowling, E. and Barnes, G. G. (2000) *Working with Children and Parents through Separation and Divorce*. Basingstoke: Palgrave Macmillan.

Mannoni, N. (1999). *Separation and Creativity: Refinding the lost language of childhood*. New York: Other Press

Mathelin, C. (1999). *Lacanian Psychotherapy with Children: The broken piano*. Trnsl. Susan Fairfield. New York: Other Press.

Milner, M. ([1934)] 1986) *A Life of One's Own*. London: Vigaro.

Sinason, V. (1992) *Mental Handicap and the Human Condition: New approaches from the Tavistock*. London: Free Association.

Warner, S. (in press) *Women and Child Sexual Abuse: Feminist revolutions in theory, research and practice*. London: Women and Psychology Series, Psychology Press.

Wilkinson, I. (1993) *Child and Family Assessment: Clinical guide for practitioners*. London: Routledge.

Winnicott, D.W. (1977) *The Piggle: An account of the psychoanalytic treatment of a little girl*. London: Penguin.

Reflexive Activity

Think of a case in which you either acted upon or rejected a child's views during assessment. What spaces did you provide the young person to express their views? What other forms of data were available in the 'social framework'? What were the points of agreement and disagreement and what proved decisive in arriving at your opinion?

---

10 ETHICS, COMMITMENT AND THE LIMITS OF ADVOCACY: PUBLIC AND PRIVATE LIVES

'The purest experiment in treatment may still be conscientious: my business is to take care of life, and to do the best for it. Science is properly more scrupulous than dogma. Dogma gives charter to mistake, and must keep the conscience alive. Alas! The scientific conscience had got into the debasing company of money, obligation and selfish respects.' Eliot ([1871–2] 1996: 606)

The author George Eliot belonged precisely to that time during the nineteenth century when the aforementioned division of labour in the sciences was articulated (that is, between the material and social sciences), resulting in further fragmentation between the medical, the psychological and the sociological domains of knowledge (see Chapter 2). Her novel, *Middlemarch*, however, contains within it many of the arguments that remain to this day as contests in ethical professional practice. Of course, she does not explore these arguments and produce any simple, handy checklist which we can pull off the shelf, but places them where they belong – in the messy lives of the human characters she creates.

There are countless references in *Middlemarch* to the links between questions of morality, intelligence and our emotional lives ('Our good depends on the quality and breadth of our emotion ...' p. 384) and many of the ensuing dilemmas which were of concern at the time are located in the character of Lydgate, the new medical 'man of science'. The way in which Lydgate deals with his very human turmoil allows us to reflect on the impossibility of severing any science that we practise from our duties and responsibilities in a social world. So, while many practitioners now look for the voice and intelligence of the young person before us in order that we show our respect for them and work in accordance with the views they express (within the spirit of Article 12; UNICEF, 1989), what do we do when our own views and professional opinion are in disagreement with those of the young person?

In this concluding chapter, therefore, I do not so much look for good practice but explore something of the messiness of case work.

OPPOSING THE VOICE OF THE CHILD

'Soniya' burst into the contact room and following the briefest of looks in my direction she literally somersaulted across the large floor space in the most fantastic gymnastic display I've ever seen. I was stunned. This had seemed like it was going to be just another case; care proceedings involving two children and their parents who were both heroin users of long-standing. Soniya's mother was heroin dependent to such a degree that she hardly knew her daughter any more, while her father by the time of this contact was living on the streets.

With the drama of her entrance, Soniya burned brightly. However, not only was she losing her parents she would also have had memories of violent events and her parents' suffering with which to cope. Furthermore, she had no friends and she struggled with reading in school, where as one can imagine she presented the most difficult of behaviours. My aim was to see what Soniya herself wanted. To some extent, of course, this was simple, for she still wanted her parents and hoped that everything would be better. But she had by now arrived at the immensely brave but rational position where she had begun to accept (at the age of eight) that her mother was in no fit state to look after her. Indeed, it seemed that Soniya had 'given up' on her mother.

On the other hand she was clearly keeping the hope alive that her father could turn things around and I hope I never forget the care and tenderness they displayed towards one another at that first contact. The mutual love and affection was not intended for prying eyes and the father exhibited such a keen emotional intellect and sensitivity that the issues of 'closeness' and 'distance' between the two were somehow so finely judged that the contact almost exhibited as a beautiful art form. Certainly he demanded and received his daughter's respect and while he had little hope of controlling her behaviour, their relationship from another point of view could be viewed as just the very best parent-child relationship possible (that is, as emotionally containing).

Clearly, Soniya still wanted to live with her father but as an addict on the streets he lived in danger, often appearing at contact having been on the receiving end of some kind of physical assault. Nevertheless, her desperation was such (for without him she was truly alone in the world) that she simply preferred to be with him wherever they might end up and in whatever conditions. The father's commitment to his daughter was such that without reservation he exhorted Soniya to co-operate with her key workers, to try hard at school and generally do what all the professionals were saying. This had become impossible for her, as her life and future had become entwined with her father's and she seemed unable to think of little else. Tragically his situation was deteriorating fast and there seemed no other course of action but to recommend that Soniya be taken permanently into care, a position with which the court could hardly disagree and which was indeed supported by her father, despite great sadness on his part. He died soon after the decision had been made.

A commitment to the children with whom we work does not mean simply accepting their views and acting upon their choices for as professionals we have a responsibility in accordance with the best interests of social government. But the story here is one of human tragedy, unfortunately replicated many thousands of times across the country. Soniya had just wanted to be with her father. He had not put her under any pressure; she had certainly not been frightened of him and neither had he encouraged her sense of reliance upon him nor her protectiveness towards him. Her reasons for wanting to be with her father were born neither out of fear of him, nor fear for him – but out of love, attachment and the weight of human feeling.

Rebecca had wanted to protect her parents but had reluctantly had to accept her own needs for safety, while Soniya's gymnastic display was analogous to her own craving for safety and containment. While Rebecca had the benefit of stable, 'good-enough' foster carers over a period of several years, Soniya had not similarly received that security and containment and her fears were out of control. Unfortunately there are many similar cases where young people can make choices which are driven by fear.

For example, in Chapter 4 I recounted something of Ben, who feared that Peter might reject him were he not to accord with his wishes. There are others who will want to stay with a parent because they fear for them, despite the risks this entails for themselves. There was a sense that Paul and Sammy (Chapters 2 and 4) had wanted to return to their mother because they feared for her and wanted to protect her; while still barely out of infants' school they had decided to take responsibility for their parent. Once again, recommendations did not simply accord with the views of the child but relied on a professional ethical response which could tolerate the dilemmas and often contradictory information.

What has gradually become clear, however, is that traditional ways of looking at children's experience (through adult eyes) and which accept as unproblematic the 'staged' models of child development – whether Piagetian, Kleinian or Eriksonian for example – invite the risk of denying various capacities which children of different ages can possess in opposition to previously accepted professional knowledge. Just as Melanie had shown a capacity for thinking and feeling supposedly beyond her years, I would suggest that the provision of the right kind of safe, containing, potential space for a child might allow for the expression of their qualities which has not traditionally been the focus for professionals. The relationships which develop while utilizing such potential space might permit safe expressions of fear or sadness but also creativity, joy and even fun.

'Bill' was caught in several dilemmas relating to home, but during my work with him he too bravely explored the space to express and communicate with me, presenting feelings about his situation but also his passion for sport. While he would engage fully he was unable to acknowledge to others, however, even in the slightest respect that he had any problems at home. His antennae for the vaguest twist in a conversation which could lead to the possibility of declaring a negative about home were keen and there was an absolute determination to remain loyal to a parent and a home situation which, despite his at times outrageous honesty during all our other work, seemed to harbour serious problems. Yet Bill did possess all sorts of abilities and I had no doubt he had the capacity not only to care for himself but for his parents too at the same time as continuing his education.

It wasn't that he was unable to understand or even distance himself from the position of others, rather that Bill seemed to have constructed an idea of himself which he either could not or would not discard, no matter what my approach or ploy. So, while having offered him a professional commitment which he seemed to welcome he did not reward me with the declaration of agreement I sought. At this point what was revealed was that my own duty and responsibility to the court (and not least my duty to protect) were in direct conflict with a professional opinion according to the expressed wishes of a young person. Once again, it is incumbent upon us to provide the burden of proof for taking a position contrary to the views of the child and I thus provided an opinion to the court contrary to Bill's expressed wishes. He had by now established his own sense of identity which was, and perhaps should be, beyond my interference.

IDENTITY AND COMMITMENT

'Mary' and 'Darren' were two young people with whom I worked over a number of years and who had long resisted those adult efforts to modify their behaviours to acceptable levels within their schools and communities, thus putting themselves in danger of being excluded from their schools. Not only this, their lives were being lived out at the boundaries of society and as such they were subject to an array of those discourses and professional interventions which work out the balances to be achieved between social cohesion, reason and order (see p. 46). I listened to the different voices of all the adults involved and the crucial discourses that seemed to emerge went something like this:

> 'Mary is not the sort of child who attends this school' (teachers)
> 'We want Mary/Darren to leave school' (teachers)
> 'We want Mary/Darren to stay at school' (respective mothers)
> 'I want to stay' (both Mary and Darren)

Discourse analysis is a coherent and systematic scientific approach which attempts to look at meanings circulated in and through (although not restricted to) language (see Lacan, 1977; Hollway, 1989; Burman and Parker, 1993; Billington, 1995 and Burman et al., 1996, for further examples and detailed application of this particular form). In piecing together a narrative which accounted for similarities in the trajectory of meanings in professional discourse, it became possible to see how the following stories had been constructed in respect of Mary and Darren:

Mary	kind of story/discourse	Darren
behaviour in school	*educational*	behaviour in school
epilepsy	*medical*	ADHD
friendless	*social*	friendless
bedwetting (SS)	*child protection*	bedwetting (SS)
peripheral father	*family*	peripheral father
poverty	*economic*	poverty
EBD school (6–11)	*other*	community violence
periods in care		'perfect' older brother

In order to work in both these cases I met individuals and groups over a period of time; listened to them, allowed/encouraged each individual to develop their own chosen narrative and always offered to return, thus making a commitment to the teachers, the parents and both Mary and Darren which went beyond usual service practices. School management was important in both cases – Mary's secondary school and Darren's primary school – for both schools operated a policy of no exclusion. In addition, it was possible eventually to identify in both schools the individual commitment of a person with power (headteacher or deputy headteacher) and gradually over a period of months new discourses began to emerge, for example that "Mary/Darren is the sort of child who attends this school."

The management of my own psychological service had also played a part, since policy was changed in such a way as to allow an individual practitioner to conduct the work and commit the time (resources) on individual cases. Such a commitment clearly had implications for other services we could provide and tough decisions had to be made regarding the extent of the work we could offer and the criteria employed for adopting a 'high-involvement' approach in just a few chosen cases.

Nevertheless the policy change permitted a more flexible response in deciding upon a committed engagement, albeit in a strictly limited number of cases. While I continued to meet with Mary, Darren, their parents and their teachers, the period between visits lengthened to every six months or so as the school staff gradually acquired the confidence to manage the behaviours of the young people and develop their own successful relationships with them. After about three years of occasional contact, Mary said that there was no need for me to see her again although I remained in contact with her teachers. Eventually, however, I was told that whilst the situation for her at home had broken down irretrievably, she had stayed at school until she was sixteen and had passed enough examinations to begin a college course. For several years, teachers at the school spoke of Mary as one of their great success stories and the strength of their relationship with her had correlated positively with the strength of their identification and commitment. Mary had become *"the sort of young person who attends our school."*

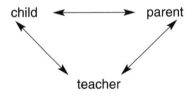

Figure 1 Reciprocal commitment

In Darren's case, he had survived at his primary school in much the same way before transferring to high school and the diagram above (see Billington, 2001) gives an idea as to the two-way connections and commitments being exhibited towards one another by the key participants, with an additional support service from myself. Unfortunately, however, his new school was a 'failing' school in which individuals with power did not commit themselves to him and meetings arranged with teachers did not materialize. For all sorts of reasons staff were reluctant to relinquish their hold on the discourse that *"Darren is not the sort of young person who we want in our school."* However, it was simply not safe for the teachers as individuals to expend the time, energy and commitment to him when their own resources had worn dangerously thin and when the systems of support, not just for pupils but for them, had virtually broken down. Under such conditions teachers were understandably reluctant to relinquish their hold on the discourse that *"Darren is not the sort of young person who we want in our school."* They were fighting for their own survival and had no spare capacity.

After just a few months, I was invited to a meeting at which the school revealed the 'deal' that had been struck with the LEA and a local secondary EBD school for boys. Darren's mother rushed out of this meeting in floods of tears while Darren sat motionless and sobbing; the headteacher became silent. I chose not to provide the reassuring noises which might have assuaged his distress and decided not to help Darren by offering continued support. I had reached the end of my own powers of commitment. Darren's social inclusion had once again correlated with the strength of identification and commitment offered by the professionals, in this case not just the teachers but the psychologist too.

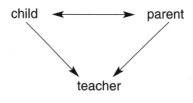

Figure 2   Reciprocal commitment severed

It was not only the teacher's commitment to the child which had broken down (Figure 2) it was also the commitment of management and support services which had failed. The social framework in both these cases saw Mary and Darren in reciprocal interactions (or otherwise) with their parents and teachers. Whenever the flow of commitment was interrupted (for example, by a parent towards the child) the young person was left potentially unsupported. My work had been to repair the flow of commitment from the teachers to Mary and also Darren. While this worked for Mary and in his primary school for Darren too, the overall strength of the social framework could support neither the commitment of his teachers nor my work as his therapist. (See also Miller and Leyden, 1999)

A year later I caught a glimpse of Darren whilst visiting someone else in his new school. His behaviour was aggressive and ugly and I no longer wanted to know him. I fear that there may be huge, long-term, economic consequences for us all as a result of Darren's social exclusion. Presumably this was a price worth paying in order to sustain the balance between social cohesion and social diversity.

ETHICAL RESOURCES

It is clearly incumbent on all those working with children to perform according to certain ethical principles and our professional bodies rightly make statements which seek to indicate the boundaries of practice (see for example British Psychological Society, 2001, 2004). That the consideration of ethical procedures and practices has achieved a much higher profile in recent years is reflected in the implementation of extra 'safeguards', not just in respect of research activity but in their application across professional domains: '... ethics at heart of courses ... Ethics will be embedded in every discipline so that all students see the relevance of ethics in the context of their disciplines or professions ...' (*Times Higher Education Supplement*, 2005). Would that it were so easy.

As suggested previously, it is clearly ethical to consult with one's clients and inform them of the processes. However, I have suggested further that our clients may possess a knowledge about themselves which will be in excess of our own. At such times we must surely invite those clients not merely to participate in their own assessments, for example, but to contribute more dynamically in the formulation of opinion. I have provided several examples of young people who were able to do just that.

But I have also provided examples of opinion in direct opposition, for example to Soniya's freely expressed wishes and feelings. While I took her views into account and did not ignore them in the processing of opinion I chose to disagree with her in the conclusion of that opinion and have done so in other cases. On what basis can I claim authority at such moments?

Evidence-based practice is yet another mantra which sounds precise and reassuringly scientific in its tone and claims to truth, but as suggested throughout this book the nature of evidence itself can be problematic. However, the researcher-practitioner model for professional work can go some way not only to ensuring that the professional has the space to keep in touch with reforming knowledge bases, but is also encouraged to develop ways of thinking about children and young people which are not overly restricted by the demands of a single employing body. Instead, the kinds of rigour usually claimed by positivist science but which are necessary for the conduct of any worthwhile research are absolutely vital in assisting hard-pressed professionals to develop the kinds of thinking which are a prerequisite for reflexive practice.

Theoretical fluency leads to more than mere introspection and on to the possibility of a confident practitioner who seeks to expand their access to knowledge and thus to a wide range of hypotheses. This will enhance an attitude to professional activities which is tolerant of the strains caused by considering the needs of children and young people quite separately from our own needs in the provision of such services. Clearly, the following three 'distinctions' are crucial in helping us to tease out the nature of the dilemmas and the basis of our position:

- between the diagnosis and the child;
- between a knowledge of children generally and our interpretations of the child before us;
- between any descriptions of the child we construct and the descriptions that the child might potentially construct for themselves.

As part of this process we have a clear responsibility to the individual child to engage with them in such a way as not to compound any harm already suffered or encountered, but rather more than this to offer them a potential space in which professional and child can meet in conditions of safety. It may be that we have to show more determination in order to create those systems of advocacy that are dedicated more precisely to representing the views of young people:

> If the development of advocacy services are to radically change policy and practice and challenge discourses which maintain the status of young people as minority group, they need to be constructed from the perspective of young people and resist construction by commissioners of services in an adult proceduralized way. (Dalrymple, 2005: 13)

Involving children and young people in accord with the principles of Article 12 (UNICEF, 1989) is subject both to support and qualification in its attempts to extend democratic potentials, for example:

> The lack of parallel provision for the development of a range of services of information consultation, support and if necessary, representation for children and young people experiencing distress and disorientation. (Timms, 2002: 223)

> Giving children a role in decisions ... was helpful in terms of their positive feelings ... Helping children to communicate their problems ... would be useful .... (Dunn and Deater-Deckard, 2001: vi)

> Children and young people were in favour of consultation which was genuine ... most of the young people we spoke to did not want to spend large amounts of time being consulted, contributing to decisions and actions. Nor did they want to be involved in taking forwards the results of consultation. This was seen as adult responsibility – children and young people have their own activities to be getting on with. (Stafford et al., 2003: 365–71).

Indeed this latter paper takes us to the boundaries of professional-child relationships for while accepting that 'children are moral agents' (Goldson et al., 2002: 87) I do not suggest we adopt this principle as an excuse for any relinquishing of adult responsibility. This has to be so especially in a culture that is susceptible to adult panic, whether on account of threats or possibilities (real or imagined). Our own adult uncertainty and insecurity are such that we too easily direct an unnecessarily intrusive and perhaps unwelcome gaze upon our young and invest them with our own fears and anxieties. Perhaps surprisingly, despite our supposed wealth of knowledge (accrued through experience but primarily unprecedented developments in technologies and science), we can begin to see that we live in a most ungrown-up society. Just as my own newborn infant had not been able to tolerate confusion or uncertainty without external comfort media frenzy seems to lurch from one crisis to another, forever reflecting a tendency towards scrutiny and surveillance ostensibly to protect but which instead inexorably places us under more searching examination and control. Frequently, these crises are then played out in our approaches to children and young people and in adult work with them, whether educational, social or therapeutic. However,

> To be at risk is to risk being alive. At any moment the consequence of being alive entails unforeseen changes which may enhance or endanger health ... Risk has now become an additional diagnosis ... (Berke, 2003: 420–1)

While not suggesting that young people are not in danger of such risks we may if we are not careful through our surveillance and scrutiny, whether official or prurient, intrude unnecessarily into the private lives of children to such a degree that in our own professional activity we constitute greater 'risk' to a young person.

There is no easy solution for we always run the risk either of responding to young people on the one hand with a professional, sanitized distance, or on the other of attempting to ignore personal defences which have been constructed for a reason. Not least there is a risk in too invasively seeking a child's stories, for can any of us trust totally our systems of government not just with our physical well-being but with our innermost thoughts and feelings? The dilemma to address, or the balance to achieve, is to acknowledge the importance of the private while not exploring it unnecessarily.

We are at the very least the co-participants in the relationships we have with our clients. Acceptance of this as science practitioners (Miller, 2006; Frederickson, 2006) or as researcher practitioners will help us to sustain the vigilance necessary to provide each young person whom we meet with that safe, potential space as part of a very special relationship.

FIVE QUESTION-THEMES – PUBLIC AND PRIVATE LIVES

So in a last return to the five question-themes, it would clearly be totally out of keeping with the approach adopted throughout this book to suddenly provide a definitive checklist of answers – how to speak of, write about, speak with or listen to the child or indeed listen to ourselves as practitioners. Instead these are offered as a resource in themselves, as questions which will never finally be resolved and which will need constantly to be addressed in each new piece of work we do, whatever our individual discipline. It may well be that the particular institutional context in which you work might require a specific application of response which is unique to your situation.

What we all share though is a working context for professional-client relationships which is changing, not only in respect of the contests between knowledge and experience, but also regarding the ownership of knowledge. Knowledge and power, of course, seem unable to escape one another and as such there is a thread running through the book which is essentially emancipatory.

This potential exists in the new spaces which are opening up in the relationships between children and adults, in our case as professionals who are employed to work with young people.

Taking account of the 'voice of the child' is clearly an important aspect of contemporary professional practice but the intention here has been not to focus on the accounts of the young people we access, but rather to reveal the problems we encounter when we attempt to implement the principle. In particular, the focus of this book has been upon us as practitioners, our practices and the theoretical assumptions which underpin our work.

The three 'distinctions' (see p 158) provided more analytical leverage since fluency in critique is vital. This is especially so, for no matter what our activity our practices with young people are interventions and demand that we are able to reflect upon the consequences of our actions. Whilst those of us who work with children should be afforded opportunities for professional supervision, as individuals we should also develop those reflexive skills which allow us to adopt the critical stance in performance of our work and as a model for professional practice – the researcher-practitioner.

While the emphasis of most professional training falls upon the nature and characteristics of our clients, I shall put forward the idea here that the effective practitioner needs some confidence that the ways in which we work with young people are harmful neither to the child nor to ourselves. The sites of our investigations, therefore, should not only be the young people but the professional relationships we share with them.

In this book I have endeavoured to answer those five question-themes not by providing unproblematic accounts of young people, but by suggesting that we have an adult responsibility to locate again our own sense of purpose and commitment. I have argued that in discovering again the value of what we do with young people we will replenish our sense of value in ourselves.

In a world in which the discourses of democracy, freedom and choice affect many of our ways of being in the world, we are left dealing with dilemmas which increasingly seem to be negotiated only at the level of the individual. Our work with children is not exempt from such processes and we are required to play out these dilemmas and anxieties, attempting to preserve social freedoms at the same time as contributing to the government of the individual. Of course, it would be more economic if the individual could assume responsibility for self-government – but this seems some way off.

The 'voice of the child' and inclusion may at some point be confined to history as mere mantra, since they take us to the sites of competing dilemmas of individual freedom of choice and public government without offering simple resolutions. Children's rights too, whilst also a site for sincere humane acts, may well increase the likelihood that as a population young people will eventually be accorded heavy responsibilities which will allow the boundaries of childhood to shift again. That we struggle to reconcile these demands in our work with children can lead too easily or inexorably to self-doubt or confusion. Indeed as professionals we may well be haunted by what has been referred to recently as 'the spectre of uselessness' (Sennett, 2006).

Ruben Gallego was born without hands and feet and with cerebral palsy. He was rejected at birth and lived in a series of orphanages and children's homes. He speaks both good and ill of his experiences but he recalls one friend saying to him 'Forgive me Ruben. You're a fine fellow and my friend, and I am glad I met you. But I wish there'd never been a children's home (Gallego, 2004: 54).

In the performance of our work with children we thus have an immense task to perform in respect of negotiating the boundaries of individual lives and experience on the one hand and the demands of government and authority on the other, for there remains that faultline between professional knowledge and individual experience. And so we are left with the question of what to do?

Perhaps social science practitioners of the future, whether psychologists, social workers, teachers or the many others working with children should be encouraged in training to rediscover those thinking skills more traditionally consigned to philosophy, history, art and literature which, of course, take us back to the roots of the social sciences in the nineteenth century. For these are traditions which can be better placed to provide resources in which we can consider not only issues of ethics and personal morality, but lessons from history, memory and experience as well as more sensitive forms of human and personal expression.

For the task we undertake when working with children is nothing less than to negotiate as part of the web of society the boundaries between the private and the public; not just in the lives of these young people but in our own.

REFERENCES

Ainsworth, M. D. S., Blehar, M. C., Waters, E. and Wells, S. (1978) *Patterns of Attachment: A psychological study of the strange situation*. Hillsdale, NJ: Erlbaum.

Alderson, P. (1995) *Listening to Children: Children, ethics and social research*. Essex: Barnardos.

Alderson, P. (2000) *Young Children's Rights: Exploring beliefs, principles and practice*. London: Jessica Kingsley Publishers.

Alexander, H., MacDonald, E. and Paton, S. (2005) Raising the issue of domestic abuse in school. *Children & Society*, 19 (3): 187–98.

Alvarez, A. (1992) *Live Company*. London: Tavistock/Routledge.

American Psychiatric Association (APA) (1994) *Diagnostic and Statistical Manual of Mental Disorders* (4th edition). DSM-IV. Washington, DC: American Psychiatric Association.

Arendt, H. (1958) *The Human Condition*. Chicago: University of Chicago Press.

Aries, P. (1962) *Centuries of Childhood*. London: Sage.

Aristotle (1976) *Ethics*. London: Penguin.

Armstrong, D. (2003) *Experiences of Special Education: Re-evaluating policy and practice through life-stories*. London: RoutledgeFalmer.

Arora, T. and Mackey, L. (2004) 'Talking and listening to children diagnosed with ADHD and taking psychostimulants' in T. Billington and M. Pomerantz (eds), *Children at the Margins*. Stoke on Trent: Trentham Books.

Association of Metropolitan Authorities (AMA) (1995) Checklist for Children: Local Authorities and the UN Convention on the Rights of the Child. *Child Care Series* 6. AMA and the Children's Rights Office.

Avdi, E., Griffiths, C. and Brough, S. (2000) Parents constructions of professional knowledge, expertise and authority during assessment and diagnosis of their child for an autistic spectrum disorder. *British Journal of Medical Psychology*, 73: 327–38.

Bailey, S. (2005) The National Service Framework: Children come of age. *Child and Adolescent Mental Health*, 10 (3):127–30.

Baron-Cohen, S., Tager-Flusberg, H. and Cohen, D. J. (eds) (1993) *Understanding Other Minds: Perspectives from autism*. Oxford: Oxford University Press.

Barton, L. (ed) (1989) *Disability and Dependency*. Sussex: Falmer.

Bate, J. (2003) 'Art in mind' in *The Reader*, 12, 7–15 (based on the script of a documentary made for BBC Radio 3).

Belsky, J. (1999) 'Interactional and contextual determinants of attachment security', in J. Cassidy and P.R. Shaver (eds), *Handbook of Attachment: Theory, research and clinical applications.* New York: Guilford.

Bene, E. and Anthony, J. (1957) *Family Relations Test: Children's version.* Windsor: NFER Nelson.

Berke, J. H. (2003) The Right to be at Risk, Free Associations 10 (4) Number 56: 420–30.

Billig, M., Condor, S., Edwards, D., Gane, M., Middleton, D. and Radley, A. (1988) *Ideological Dilemmas: A social psychology of everyday thinking.* London: Sage.

Billington, T. (1995) Discourse Analysis: Acknowledging interpretation in everyday practice. *Educational Psychology in Practice,* 11 (3): 36–45.

Billington, T. (1996) 'Pathologizing Children: Psychology in education and acts of government', in E. Burman, G. Aitken, P. Alldred, R. Allwood, R. T. Billington, B. Goldberg, A. J. Gordo Lopez, C. Hennan, D. Marks and S. Warner (eds), *Psychology Discourse Practice: Regulation and resistance.* London: Taylor and Francis.

Billington, T. (1999) Feminist questions, educational psychology and discourses of difference. *Educational and Child Psychology,* 16 (2): 27–34.

Billington, T. (2000a) *Separating, Losing and Excluding Children: Narratives of difference.* London: Routledge Falmer.

Billington, T. (2000b) 'Words, pathologies and children', in M. Moore (ed.), *Insider Perspectives on Inclusion: Raising voices, raising issues.* Sheffield: Philip Armstrong Publications. pp. 81–93.

Billington, T. (2000c) Autistic Spectrum Disorders: Interim Report. *Metropolitan Borough of Wirral.* March.

Billington, T. (2001) Autistic Spectrum Disorders: Children's emotional lives. *Metropolitan Borough of Wirral.* June and December.

Billington, T. (2002) Children, Psychologists and Knowledge: A discourse-analytic narrative. *Educational and Child Psychology,* 19 (3): 32–41.

Billington, T. (2003) Narrative work with children and young people (unpublished paper), University of Sheffield, Group for the Advanced Study and Practice of Educational Psychology. December.

Billington, T. (2004) 'Re-presenting Callum', in T. Billington and M. Pomerantz (eds), *Children at the Margins: Supporting children, supporting schools.* Stoke on Trent: Trentham Books.

Billington, T. (2006) Review Essay: Autism: Speculation, knowledge or understanding? *Discourse: Studies in the Cultural Politics of Education,* 27 (2).

Billington, T. and Pomerantz, M. (eds) (2004) *Children at the Margins: Supporting children, supporting schools.* Stoke on Trent: Trentham Books.

Billington, T. and Warner, S. (eds) (2003) Editorial in Child Protection: Theory, research and practice. *Educational and Child Psychology,* 20 (1): 4–6.

Billington, T., McNally, B. and McNally, C. (2000) Autism: Working with parents, and discourse in experience, expertise and learning. *Educational Psychology in Practice,* 16 (1): 59–68.

Binet, A. and Simon, T. (1905) New methods for diagnosis of the intellectual level of subnormals. *L'Année Psychologique,* 14: 1–90.

Bion, W. R. (1961) *Experiences in Groups*. London: Tavistock.

Bion, W. R. (1962) *Learning from Experience*. London: William Heinemann Medical Books.

Bion, W. R. (1970) *Attention and Interpretation*. London: Tavistock.

Bird, L. (2002) Feminist questions about children's competence. *Education and Child Psychology*, 16 (2): 17–26.

Boucher, J. (1996) 'The inner life of children with autistic difficulties', in V. Varma (ed.), *The Inner Life of Children with Special Educational Needs*. London: Whurr.

Bourdieu, P. (1990) *Reproduction in Education, Society and Culture (Theory, Culture and Society)*. London: Sage.

Bowlby, J. (1969) *Attachment and Loss* (Volume One: *Attachment*) London: Hogarth Press.

Bowlby, J. (1988) *A Secure Base: Clinical applications of attachment theory*. London: Routledge.

Bowlby, J. (1994) *The Making and Breaking of Affectional Bonds*. London: Routledge.

British Psychological Society (BPS) (2001) *Child Abuse – Clinical Factors in the Assessment and Management of Concern*. London: Division of Clinical Psychology BPS.

British Psychological Society (BPS) (2004) *Child Protection: Safeguarding Children and Young People from Abuse, Harm and Neglect: The responsibilities of chartered psychologists*. London: BPS.

British Psychological Society (BPS) (forthcoming) *Autistic Specturm Disorders: guidance for chartered psychologists working with children and young people*. London: BPS.

Brown, W. (1922). In. W. Whately Smith. *The Measurement of Emotion*. London: Kegan Paul, Trench, Trubner and Co. Ltd

Bruner, J. (1986) *Actual Minds: Possible Worlds*. Harvard: Harvard University Press.

Bruner, J. and Haste, H. (eds) (1990) *Making Sense: The child's construction of the world*. London: Routledge.

Burman, E. (1994) *Deconstructing Developmental Psychology*. London: Routledge.

Burman, E. (1997a) Telling Stories: Psychologists, children and the production of 'false memories'. *Theory and Psychology*, 7 (3): 291–309.

Burman, E. (1997b) 'Developmental psychology and its discontents', in D. Fox and I. Prilleltensky (eds), *Critical Psychology: An introduction*. London: Sage.

Burman, E. (1999) Feminist questions about children's competence. *Educational and Child Psychology*, 16 (2): 17–26.

Burman, E. (2001) Emotions in the classroom: and the institutionalised politics of knowledge. *Psychoanalytic Studies*, 3 and 4: 313–24.

Burman, E. and Parker, I. (eds) (1993) *Discourse Analytic Research: Repertoires and readings of texts in action*. London: Routledge.

Burman, E., Alldred, P., Bewley, C., Goldberg, B., Heenan, C., Marks, D., Marshall, J., Taylor, K., Ullah, R. and Warner, S. (1996) *Challenging Women:*

Psychology's exclusions, feminist possibilities. Buckingham: Open University Press.

Carr, W. (1998) The curriculum in and for a democratic society. *Curriculum Studies*, 6 (3): 323–40.

Chailey Heritage (1992) *Guidelines and Policies Relating to Child Protection.* Sussex: Chailey Heritage Working Group

Chomsky, N. (1986) *Knowledge of Language.* New York: Praeger.

Cleaver, H., Unell, I. and Aldgate, J. (1999) *Children's Needs – Parenting Capacity: The impact of parental mental illness, problem alcohol and drug use, and domestic violence on children's development.* Norwich: HMSO.

Clough, P. and Barton, L. (1995) *Making Difficulties.* London: Paul Chapman.

Clough, P. and Barton, L. (1998) *Articulating with Difficulty: Research voices in inclusive education.* London: Paul Chapman.

Collier, P. (1994) Child protection, children's rights and the 1981 Education Act. *DECP Newsletter* 35–8.

Cooter, R. (ed.) (1992) *In the Name of the Child.* London: Routledge.

Cullen, K. and Shaldon, C. (2003) Learning to read: children's emotional experience. *Educational and Child Psychology*, 20 (4): 15–40.

Dallos, R. and Draper, R. (2000) *An Introduction to Family Therapy.* Berkshire: Open University Press.

Dalrymple, J. (2005) Constructions of child and youth advocacy: emerging issues in advocacy practice. *Children & Society*, 19 (1): 3–15.

Damasio, A. (1994) *Descartes' Error: Emotion, reason and the human brain.* New York: Quill.

Damasio, A. (2000) *The Feeling of What Happens: Body emotion and the making of consciousness.* London: Vintage.

Damasio, A. (2001) Reflections on the Neurobiology of Function and Feeling, *The Foundations of Cognitive Science.* Oxford: Oxford University Press.

Damasio, A. (2004) *Looking for Spinoza: Joy, sorrow and the feeling brain.* London: Vintage.

Davis, P. (2002) *The Victorians: Oxford English Literary History* (Vol. 8, 1830–1880). Oxford: Oxford University Press.

Department for Education and Employment (DfEE) (1993) *Education Act.* London: HMSO.

Department for Education and Employment (DfEE) (1994) *The Code of Practice and Special Educational Needs.* London: HMSO.

Department for Education and Employment (DfEE) (1995) *Protecting Children from Abuse: The role of the education service* (Circular 10/95). London: DfEE Publications.

Department for Education and Employment (DfEE) (1998a) *Meeting Special Educational Needs: A programme of action.* Suffolk: DfEE Publications.

Department for Education and Employment (DfEE) (1998b) *The National Teaching Strategy: A framework for teaching.* London: DfEE Publications.

Department for Education and Science (DfES) (1978) *Warnock Report.* London: HMSO.

Department for Education and Science (DfES) (1981) *The Education Act.* London: HMSO.

Department for Education and Skills (DfES) (2001) *Special Educational Needs and Disability Rights Act*. Nottingham: DfES Publications.

Department for Education and Skills (DfES) (2002) *Education Act*. London: HMSO.

Department for Education and Skills (DfES) (2003) *The Green Paper: Every Child Matters*. Norwich:HMSO.

Department for Education and Skills (DfES) (2004) *Every Child Matters: Change for children*. Nottingham: DfES Publications.

Department for Education and Skills (DfES) (2005) *Common Assessment Framework for Children and Young People: Guide for service managers and practitioners*. Nottingham: DfES Publications.

Department for Education and Skills and Department of Health (DfES/DoH) (2004) *The National Service Framework for Children, Young People and Maternity Services*. London: Department of Health.

Department of Health (DoH) (1991) *The Children Act 1989*. London: HMSO.

Department of Health (DoH) (1995) *Child Protection: Messages from Research*. London: HMSO.

Department of Health (DoH) (1998a) *Modernising Social Services: Promoting independence, improving protection, raising standards*. London:HMSO.

Department of Health (DoH) (1998b) *Working Together to Safeguard Children: Consultation paper*. Wetherby: Department of Health.

Department of Health (DoH) (1998c) *People Like Us: The report of the review of the Safeguards for Children Living Away from Home* (Utting Report). London: HMSO.

Department of Health (DoH) (2000) *Framework for the Assessment of Children in Need and their Families*. London: HMSO.

Department of Health (DoH) (2001a) *Studies informing the Framework for the Assessment of Children in Need and their Families*. London: HMSO.

Department of Health (DoH) (2001b) *The Children Act Now: Messages From Research: Studies in evaluating the Children Act 1989*. London: HMSO.

Department of Health (DoH) (2002) *Safeguarding Children: Joint Chief Inspectors' Report on Arrangements to Safeguard Children*. London: HMSO.

Department of Health and Department for Education and Employment (2000) *Framework for the Assessment of Children in Need and their Families*. London: HMSO.

Derrida, J. (1975) The Purveyor of truth. *Yale French Studies*, 52: 31–113.

Derrida, J. (1978) *Writing and Difference*. London: Routledge & Kegan Paul.

Descartes, R. (1637) *Discourse de la Methode*.

DeShazer, S. (1988) *Clues: Investigating solutions in brief therapy*. New York: Norton.

Dixon, L., Browne, K. and Hamilton-Giachritsis, C. (2005a) Risk factors of parents abused as children: a mediational analysis of the intergenerational continuity of child maltreatment (Part I). *Journal of Child Psychology and Psychiatry*, 46 (1): 47–57.

Dixon, L., Hamilton-Giachritis, C. and Browne, K. (2005b) Attributions and behaviours of parents abused as children: a mediational analysis of the intergenerational continuity of child maltreatment (Part II). *Journal of Child Psychology and Psychiatry*, (46) (1): 47–57.

Dominelli, L. (2004) *Social Work: Theory and practice for a changing profession.* Cambridge: Polity.

Donaldson, M. (1978) *Children's Minds.* London: Fontana.

Dowling, E. and Barnes, G. G. (2000) *Working with Children and Parents through Separation and Divorce.* Basingstoke: Palgrave Macmillan.

Dowling, E. and Osborne, E. (1985) *The Family and the School: A joint systems approach to problems with children.* London: Routledge and Kegan Paul.

Duden, B. (1992) in W. Sachs. (ed.) *The Development Dictionary: A guide to knowledge as power.* London: Zed.

Dunn, J. (2004) *Children's Friendships: The beginnings of intimacy.* Oxford: Blackwell.

Dunn, J. and Deater -Deckard, K. (2001) *Children's Views of their Changing Families.* York: Joseph Rowntree Foundation.

Durig, A. (1996) *Autism and the Crisis of Meaning.* New York: State University of New York Press.

Eliot, G. ([1871–2] 1996) *Middlemarch.* London: Oxford University Press.

Erikson, E. ([1991] 1995) *Childhood and Society.* London: Vintage.

Every Child Matters (2005) *CAF for children and young people: Guide for Service Managers and practitioners.* Accessed March 2005 at www. everychildmatters.gov. uk/deliveringservices/caf/

Fonagy, P. (2001) *Attachment Theory and Psychoanalysis.* New York: Other.

Foucault, M. (1967) *Madness and Civilisation.* London: Routledge.

Foucault, M. (1970) *The Order of Things.* London: Tavistock.

Foucault, M. (1972) *The Archaeology of Knowledge.* London: Tavistock.

Foucault, M. (1977) *Discipline and Punish: The birth of the prison.* London: Allen Lane.

Foucault, M. (1979) 'On Governmentality' *Ideology and Consciousness*, 6: 5–21.

Foulkes, S.H. (1964) *Therapeutic London Group Analysis.* London: George Allen and Unwin.

France, A. and Utting, D. (eds) (2005) The paradigm of 'Risk and Protection-Focused Prevention' and its impact on services for children and families. *Children and Society*, 19 (2): 77–90.

Frederickson, N. (2006) *A modern re-conceptualisation of educational psychologists as scientist practitioners: identifying the distinctive contribution.* Presented at the British Psychological Society: Division of Educational and Child Psychology Annual Conference. Bournemouth, 5 January.

Freiberg, K., Homel, R., Batchelor, S., Carr, A., Hay, I., Elias, G., Teague, R. and Lamb, C. (2005) Pathways to Participation: A community-based developmental prevention project in Australia. *Children & Society*, 19 (2): 144–57.

Frith, U. (1989) *Autism: Explaining the enigma.* Oxford: Blackwell.

Frith, U. (2003) *Autism: The enigma.* Cambridge: Cambridge University Press.

Freud, S. ([1900] 1976) *The Interpretation of Dreams.* London: Pelican.

Freud, S. ([1915–17] 1973) *Introductory Lectures in Psychoanalysis*. London: Penguin.

Freud, S. ([1920] 1984) Beyond the Pleasure Principle. *On Metapyschology*. London: Penguin.

Fromm, E. ([1942] 1984) *The Fear of Freedom*. London: Ark.

Frosh, S. (1987) *The Politics of Psychoanalysis*. Basingstoke: Macmillan Education.

Frosh, S. (1989) *Psychoanalysis and Psychology*. Basingstoke: Macmillan Education.

Gallego, R. (2006) *White on Black* (transl. Marion Schwarh). London: John Murray.

Galton, M. ([1869] 1892, 2nd Edition) *Hereditary Genius: an inquiry into its laws and consequences*. London: Macmillan and Co.

Galton, M. ([1883] *Inquiries into Human Faculty and Development*. London: Macmillan and Co.

Gardner, H. (1983) *Frames of Mind*. London: Paladin.

Genette, G. (1980) *Narrative Discourse* (transl. E. Lewin). Oxford: Blackwell.

Georgaca, E. (1995) *Things Beyond Language? Lacan and Kristeva*. Presentation at the Discourse Unit: Manchester Metropolitan University.

Gillberg, I. C. and Gillberg, C. (1989) Asperger's Syndrome: some epidemiological considerations. *Journal of Child Psychology and Psychiatry*, 30: 631–38.

Goldson, B., Lavalette, M. and McKechnie, J. (2002) *Children, Welfare and the State*. London: Sage.

Goleman, D. (1995) *Emotional Intelligence*. New York: Bantam.

Goodenough, T., Williamson, E., Kent, J. and Ashcroft, R. (2003) 'What Did You Think About That?' Researching children's perceptions of participation in a longitudinal genetic epidemiological study. *Children & Society*, 17 (2): 113–25.

Goodley, D. and Lawthom, R. (eds) (2006) *Disability and Psychology: Critical introductions and reflections*. Basingstoke: Palgrave Macmillan.

Grandin, T. and Scariano, M. M. (1986) *Emergence: Labelled autistic*. Novato, CA: Arena Press.

Green, J. and D'Oliveira, M. (1982) *Learning to Use Statistical Tests in Psychology*. Buckingham: Open University Press.

Griffiths, F. (2002) *Communication Counts*. London: David Fulton.

Hall, K. (2001) *Asperger's Syndrome, The University and Everything*. London: Jessica Kingsley.

Happe, F. (1999) Understanding assets and deficits in autism: why success is more interesting than failure. *The Psychologist*, 12 (11): 540–46.

Henriques, J., Hollway, W., Urwin, C., Venn, C. and Walkerdine, V. (1984) *Changing the Subject*. London: Methuen.

Hesmondhalgh, M. and Breakey, C. (2001) *Access and Inclusion for Children with Autistic Spectrum Disorders: 'Let me in'*. London: Jessica Kingsley.

Hill, M. (ed.) (1999) *Effective Ways of Working with Children and their Families*. London: Jessica Kingsley.

Hill, M. and Kay, T. (1997) *Children and Society*. London: Longman.

Hinshelwood, R. (1994) *Clinical Klein.* London: Free Association.

HMSO (1989) *The Children Act.* London: HMSO.

HMSO (2001) *Special Educational Needs and Disability Act.* London: The Stationary Office.

Hoagwood, K. E. (2005) Family-based services in children's mental health: a research review and synthesis. *Journal of Child Psychology and Psychiatry,* 46 (7): 690–713.

Hobsbawm, E. J. (1962) *The Age of Revolution 1789–1848.* London: Sphere.

Hobsbawm, E. J. (1975) *The Age of Capital 1848–1875.* London: Abacus.

Hobsbawm, E. J. (1987) *The Age of Empire 1875–1914.* London: Abacus.

Hobsbawm, E.J. (1995) *The Age of Extremes.* London: Abacus.

Hobson, P. (2002) *The Cradle of Thought: Exploring the origins of thinking.* London: Macmillan.

Hollway, W. (1989) *Subjectivity and Method in Psychology.* London: Sage.

Hollway, W. and Jefferson, T. (2000) *Doing Qualitative Research Differently.* London: Sage.

Howe, D., Brandon, M., Hinings, D. and Schofield, G. (1999) *Attachment Theory, Child Maltreatment and Family support: A practice and assessment model.* London: Palgrave.

James, A. and Prout, A. (1997) *Constructing and Reconstructing Childhood: Contemporary issues in the sociological study of childhood.* (2nd edn.) London: Falmer.

James, A., Jenks, C. and Prout, A. (1998) *Theorizing Childhood.* Cambridge: Polity.

James, W. (1890) *The Principles of Psychology* (Volumes I and II). New York: Henry Holt.

James, W. ([1902] 1982) *The Varieties of Religious Experience.* London: Penguin.

James, W. (1980) *The Principles of Psychology.* New York: Holt, Rinehart and Winston.

Jenkins, R. (1998) 'Towards a social model of (in) competence', in R. Jenkins (ed.), *Questions of Competence.* Buckingham: Open University Press.

Johnson, T. (1972) *Professions and Power.* Basingstoke: MacMillan Education

Jolliffe, T., Lansdown, R. and Robinson, C. (1992) Autism: a personal account. *Communication,* 26 (3): 12–19.

Jonkman, H, B., Junger-Tas, J. and van Dijk, B. (2005) From behind dikes and dunes: communities that care in the Netherlands. *Children & Society,* 19 (2): 105–16.

Jordan, B. (2001) Tough love: social work, social exclusion and the Third Way. *British Journal of Social Work,* 31: 527–46.

Jordan, R., Jones, G. and Murray, D. (1998) *Educational Interventions for Children with Autism: A literature review of recent and current research.* (Report 77). DfEE

Joseph, B. (1988) in E. B. Spillius (ed.), *Melanie Klein Today* Vol.1: *Mainly Theory.* London: Routledge.

Juffer, F., Bakermans-Kranenburg, M. J. and van Ijzendoorn, M. H. (2005) The importance of parenting in the development of disorganized attachment: evidence from a preventive intervention study in adoptive families. *Journal of Child Psychology and Psychiatry*, 46 (3): 263–74.

Jung, C. G. (1957) *The Undiscovered Self*. Zurich: Rascher.

Kearney, R. (2002) *On Stories*. London: Routledge.

Kelly, G. (1955) *The Psychology of Personal Construct*. New York: Norton.

Klein, M. (1932) *The Psychoanalysis of Children*. London: Hogarth.

Klein, M. ([1957] 1988) *Envy and Gratitude and Other Works 1946–1963*. London: Virago.

Kolko, D. J. and Kazdin, A. E. (1993) Emotional/behavioural problems in clinic and nonclinic children: correspondence among children, parent and teacher reports. *Journal of Child Psychology and Psychiatry*, 34: 991–1006.

Kranowitz, C. S. (1998) *The out-of-sync Child: Recognising and coping with sensory integration dysfunction*. New York: Perigree.

Lacan, J. (1977) *Ecrits: A Selection*. London: Routledge.

Laing, R. D. (1960) *The Divided Self*. London: Penguin.

Laing, R. D. (1961) *Self and Others*. London: Penguin.

Laming, Lord (2003) *The Victoria Climbie Inquiry*. London: HMSO.

Lansdown, G. (1995) *Taking Part: Children's participation in decision-making*. London: IPRR.

Laplanche, J. and Pontalis, J.-B. (1973) *The Language of Psychoanalysis*. London: Karnac.

Law, I. (1997) Attention Deficit Disorder: Therapy with a shoddily built construct, in C. Smith and D. Nylund (eds), *Narrative Therapies with Children and Adolescents*. New York: Guilford.

Leach, R. (2003) Children's participation in family decision-making. National Children's Bureau. *Highlight*, 196.

Levette, A. (1995) Stigmatic factors in sexual abuse and the violence of representation. *Psychology in Society*, 20: 4–12.

Lewin, K. (1948) *Resolving Social Conflicts: Selected Papers on Group Dynamics*. New York: Harper and Row.

Lloyd-Bennett, P. and Billington, T. (eds) (2001) Multidisciplinary work for children with autism. *Educational and Child Psychology*, Special Issue, 18 (2).

Lukacs, G. ([1937] 1962) *The Historical Novel* (transl H. Mitchell). London: Merlin.

Lyon, C. (2003) *Child Abuse* (third edn.) Bristol: Jordan.

MacIntrye, A. (1967) *A Short History of Ethics*. London: Routledge & Kegan Paul.

MacIntyre, A. (1981) *After Virtue: A study in moral theory*. London: Duckworth.

Mannoni, N. (1999) *Separation and Creativity: Refinding the lost language of childhood*. New York: Other Press.

Marchant, R. and Waller, L. (1992) 'Chailey heritage: a chapter of children's rights', in R. Marchant and R. Pemberton (eds), *What's the Difference? The challenge of child protection work with disabled children* (Report of cross Sussex multi-agency conference).

Mathelin, C. (1999) *Lancanian Psychotherapy with Children: The Broken Piano*. Transl. Susan Fairfield. New York: Other Press.

Matthews, G. B. (1984) *Dialogues with Children*. Cambridge, MA: Harvard University Press.

Matthews, H. (2003) Children and regeneration: setting an agenda for community participation and integration. *Children and Society*, 17 (4): 264–76.

Mayall, B. (1996) *Children, Health and Social Order*. Buckingham: Open University Press.

Mayall, B. (2002) *Towards a Sociology for Childhood: Thinking from children's lives*. Buckingham: Open University Press.

McDermott, R. P. (1993) *The acquisition of a child by a learning disability,* in J. Lave and S. Chaiklin (eds), *Understanding Practice: Perspectives on activity and context*. New York: Cambridge University Press. pp. 269–305.

McKecknie, J. (2002) Children's voices and researching childhood, in B., Goldson, M. Lavalette, and J. McKecknie (eds), *Children, Welfare and the State*. London: Sage.

Mill, J. S. ([1859] 1869) *On Liberty*. London: Longman, Roberts and Green.

Miller, A. (2006) Original conceptualisations of educational psychologists as scientist-practitioners: promises and pitfalls. Presented at the British Psychological Society: Division of Educational and Child Psychology, Bournemouth, 5 January.

Miller, A. and Leyden, G. (1999) A coherent framework for the application of psychology in schools. *British Educational Research Journal*, 25 (3) 389–400.

Miller, S. (2000) Researching children: issues arising from a phenomenological study with children who have diabetes mellitus. *Journal of Advanced Nursing*, 31 (5): 1228–34.

Milner, M. ([1934] 1986) *A Life of One's Own*. London: Vigaro.

Mitchell, J. (2003) *Siblings*. Cambridge: Polity.

Moore, M. (ed.) (2000) *Insider Perspectives on Inclusion: Raising voices, raising issues*. Sheffield: Philip Armstrong.

Morgan, A. (2000) *What is Narrative Therapy?* Accessd at http://www.dulwichcentre. com.au/alicearticle html, December 2003.

Morris, J. (2003) Including all children: finding out about the experiences of children with communication and/or cognitive impairments. *Children & Society*, 17 (5): 337–48.

Nagel, T. (1979) *Mortal Questions*. Cambridge: Cambridge University Press.

Nagel, T. (1986) *The View from Nowhere*. Oxford: Oxford University Press.

Newman, F. and Holzman, L. (1993) *Lev Vygotsky: Revolutionary scientist*. London: Routledge.

Nightingale, D. and Cronby, J. (eds) (1999) *Social Constructionist Psychology and Critical Analyses of Theory and Practice*. Buckingham: Open University Press.

Owen, R. ([1813] 1927) *A New View of Society*. London: Dent.

Pansini, G. (1997) The structure of internal space: conditions for change in a 6 year old girl with severe developmental delay. *Journal of Child Psychotherapy*, 23 (1): 25–50.

Parker, I. (1992). *Discourse Dynamics*. London: Routledge.

Parker, I. (2005) *Qualitative Psychology: Introducing radical research*. Berkshire: Open University Press.

Parker, I. and Spears, R. (eds) (1996) *Psychology and Society*. London: Pluto.

Parker, I., Georgaca, E., Harper, D., McLaughlin, T. and Stowell-Smith, M. (1995) *Deconstructing Psychopathology*. London: Sage.

Parton, N. (1991) *Governing the Family: Child care, child protection and the state*. Basingstoke: Macmillan.

Perls, F., Hefferline, R. F. and Goodman, P. (1951) *Gestalt Therapy: Excitement and growth in the human personality*. London: Souvenir.

Phoenix, A. (1997) The Place of 'race' and ethnicity in the lives of children and young people. *Educational and Child Psychology*, 14 (3): 5–24.

Piaget, J. (1936) *The Origins of Intelligence in the Child*. London: Routledge & Kegan Paul.

Piontelli, A. (1992) *From Fetus to Child*. London: Routledge.

Popper, K. R. (1966*) Logik de Forsching* (2nd edn). Tubingen: Unbekannter Verlag.

Raitt, F. E. and Zeedyk, M. S. (2000) *The Implicit Relation of Psychology and Law: Women and syndrome evidence*. London: Routledge.

Renough, A.G. and Kovacs, M. (1994) Concordance between mothers' reports and children's self reports of depressive symptoms: a longitudinal study. *Journal of the American Academy of Child and Adolescent Psychiatry*, 33: 208–16.

Riley, D. (1983) *War in the Nursery*. London: Virago.

Rogers, C.R. (1951) *Client-Centred Counselling*. Boston: Houghton-Mifflin.

Roker, D. and Eden, K. (2003) Taking 'social action': how some British young people are bringing about change in society. *Representing Children*, 16 (1): 31–46.

Rose, N. (1985) *The Psychological Complex*. London: Routledge & Kegan Paul.

Rose, N. (1989) *Governing the Soul: The shaping of the private self*. London: Routledge.

Rose, N. and Miller, P. (1992) Political power beyond the state: problematics of government. *British Journal of Sociology*, 43 (2) June:

Roth, A. and Fonagy, P. (1996) *What Works for Whom? A critical review of psychotherapy research*. New York: Guilford.

Rutter, M. (2002) A Combination Still to Crack! *Times Higher Education Supplement*, 29 March, 15.

Rutter, M., Tizard, J. and Whitmore, K. (eds) (1970) *Education, Health and Behaviour*. London: Longmans.

Ryle, G. (1949) *The Concept of Mind*. London: Penguin.

Sacks, O. (1985) *The Man Who Mistook His Wife for a Hat*. London: Picador.

Sacks, O. (2004) *Vintage Sacks*. New York: Vintage.

Sainsbury, C. (2000) *Martian in the Playground: Understanding the school child with Asperger's Syndrome*. Bristol: Lucky Duck.

Saussure, F. de (1964) *Course in General Linguistics*. London: Fontana.

Sedgwick, F. (1990) *Thinking About Literacy*. London: Routledge.

Segal, H. (1986) *Notes on symbolic formation in the Works of Hanna Segal: Delusion and autistic creativity and other psychoanalytic essays.* London: Free Association.

Sennett, R. (2006) *The Culture of the New Capitalism.* New Haven, CT: Yale University Press.

Shaldon, C. and Cullen, K. (2003) Learning to read children's emotional experience. *Educational and Child Psychology,* 20 (4): 15–40.

Sheir, H. (2001) Pathways to participation: openings opportunities and obligations: a new model for enhancing children's participation in decision-making, in line with Article 12.1 of the UN Convention on the Rights of the Child. *Children and Society,* 15: 107–17.

Shepherd, M., Watt, D., Falloon, I. and Smeeton, N. (1989) The natural history of schizophrenia: A five year follow-up of outcome and prediction in a representative sample of schizophrenics. *Psychological Medicine Monograph 16.* Cambridge: Cambridge University Press.

Shotter, J. (1990) Social individuality versus possessive individualism, in I. Parker and J. Shotter (eds), *Deconstructing Social Psychology,* London: Routledge.

Shotter, J. and Parker, I. (eds) (1990) *Deconstructing Social Psychology.* London: Routledge.

Sinason, V. (1988) Smiling, swallowing, sickening and stupefying: the effect of sexual abuse on the child. *Psychoanalytical Psychotherapy,* 3 (2): 97–111.

Sinason, V. (1992) *Mental Handicap and the Human Condition: New approaches from the Tavistock.* London: Free Association.

Sinclair, J. (2004) website at http://www.angelfire.com/in/AspergerArtforms/autism. html

Smith, C. and Nylund, D. (1997) *Narrative Therapies with Children and Adolescents.* New York: Guilford.

Spearman, C. (1904) 'General Intelligence' objectively determined and measured. *American Journal of Psychology,* 15: 201–93.

Spencer, H. (1876) *The Principles of Sociology* (Volume One). London: Williams and Norgate.

Spencer, H. ([1861] 1932) *Education.* Cambridge: Cambridge University Press.

Spencer, H. (1900) *First Principles.* New York: Collier.

Spender, D. (1989) *Invisible Women: The schooling scandal.* London: The Women's Press.

Spinoza, B. ([1677] 1989) *Ethics.* London: Dent.

Stafford, A., Laybourn, A. and Hill, M. (2003) 'Having a Say': children and young people talk about consultation. *Children & Society,* 17 (5): 361–73.

Stern, D. (1985) *The Interpersonal World of the Infant: A view from psychoanalysis and developmental psychology.* New York: Basic.

Sullivan, H. S. (1964) *The Fusion of Psychiatry and Social Science.* New York: Norton.

Sullivan, J. (2006) *Woman's Hour.* BBC Radio Four: 23 January.

Timimi, S. (2004) Beyond Nature *v.* Nurture. *Asylum,* 14 (2): 20–1.

Timms, J. (1996) *Practice in Progress: Skills and dilemmas – messages from practice.* The Welsh Office (Department of Health).

Timms, J. (2002) The Adoption and Children Act 2002 Part 2: Amendments to the Children Act 1989 – implications for the Representation of Children Act 1989. *Representing Children,* 15 (4): 215–40.

Tolman, C. W. (1994) *Psychology, Society and Subjectivity.* London: Routledge.

Tomasello, M. (1999) *The Cultural Origins of Human Cognition.* Cambridge: Harvard University Press.

Turton, M. (1997) Personal communication.

UNESCO (1994) *The Salamanca Statement and the Framework for Action on Special Needs Education.* Paris: UNESCO.

UNICEF (1989) UN Convention on the Rights of the Child. Geneva: Office of the High Commissioner for Human Rights. Unicef.

Urwin, C. and Sharland, E. (1992) From bodies to minds in childcare literature, in P. Cooper. (ed.), *In the Name of the Child.* London: Routledge.

Varma, V. P. (ed.) (1992) *The Secret Life of Vulnerable Children.* London: Routledge.

Vygotsky, L. S. (1978) *Mind in Society.* London: Harvard University Press.

Vygotsky, L. S. (1986) *Thought and Language.* Cambridge, MA: Harvard University Press.

Wagner, P. (2000) Consultation: developing a comprehensive approach to service delivery. *Educational Psychology in Practice.* 16 (1): 9–18.

Wall, N. (2000) *A Handbook for Expert Witnesses in Children Act Cases.* Bristol: Family Law.

Warner, F. (1897) *The Study of Children.* London: Macmillan.

Warner, S. (2000) *Understanding Child Sexual Abuse: Making the Tactics Visible.* Gloucester: Handsell.

Warner, S. (in press) *Women and Child Sexual Abuse: Feminist revolutions in theory, research and practice.* London: Psychology Press.

Waterman, A., Blades, M. and Spencer, C. P. (2000) Children's comprehension of questions, in H. Westcott, E. Davis and R. Bull (eds.), *Children's Testimony: Psychological research and forensic practice.* Chichester: Wiley.

White, M. (1989) The externalising of the problem and the re-authoring of lives and relationships: externalizing the problem. *Dulwich Centre Newsletter,* Summer 1988–1989.

White, M. and Epston, D. (1990) *Narrative Means to Therapeutic Ends.* Adelaide: Dulwich Centre.

Wilkinson, I. (1993) *Child and Family Assessment: Clinical guide for practitioners.* London: Routledge.

Williams, D. (1992) *Nobody Nowhere.* London: Doubleday.

Williams, D. (1996) *Autism: An inside out approach.* London: Jessica Kingsley.

Williams, R. (1976) *Keywords.* London: Fontana.

Williams, R. (1987) *Culture and Society.* London: Fonagy.

Wing, L. (1996) *The Autistic Spectrum.* London: Constable

Winnicott, D. W. (1971) *Playing and Reality.* Tavistock.

Winnicott, D. W. (1977) *The Piggle: An account of the psychoanalytic treatment of a little girl.* London: Penguin.

Wittgenstein, L. (1953) *Philosophical Investigations.* Oxford: Blackwell.

Wood, D. J., Bruner, J. S. and Ross, G. (1976) The role of tutoring in problem-solving. *Journal of Child Psychology and Psychiatry*, 17: 89–100.

Woodhead, M. (1999) Deconstructing developmental psychology. *Children and Society*, 13: 3–19.

Young, R. (1989) 'Transitional phenomena: production and consumption', in B. Richards, (ed.), *Crises of the Self: Further essays - psychoanalysis and politics.* London: Free Association.

INDEX